Statistics for HCI
Making Sense of Quantitative Data

Synthesis Lectures on Human-Centered Informatics

Editor
John M. Carroll, *Penn State University*

Human-Centered Informatics (HCI) is the intersection of the cultural, the social, the cognitive, and the aesthetic with computing and information technology. It encompasses a huge range of issues, theories, technologies, designs, tools, environments and human experiences in knowledge, work, recreation and leisure activity, teaching and learning, and the potpourri of everyday life. The series publishes state-of-the-art syntheses, case studies, and tutorials in key areas. It shares the focus of leading international conferences in HCI.

Statistics for HCI: Making Sense of Quantitative Data

Alan Dix

ISBN: 978-3-031-01100-9   paperback
ISBN: 978-3-031-02228-9   ebook
ISBN: 978-3-031-00208-3   hardcover

DOI 10.1007/978-3-031-02228-9

A Publication in the Springer series
SYNTHESIS LECTURES ON HUMAN-CENTERED INFORMATICS

Lecture #44
Series Editor: John M. Carroll, *Penn State University*
Series ISSN
Print 1946-7680   Electronic 1946-7699

Statistics for HCI

Making Sense of Quantitative Data

Alan Dix
Computational Foundry, Swansea University, Wales

SYNTHESIS LECTURES ON HUMAN-CENTERED INFORMATICS #44

ABSTRACT

Many people find statistics confusing, and perhaps even more confusing given recent publicity about problems with traditional p-values and alternative statistical techniques including confidence intervals and Bayesian statistics. This book aims to help readers navigate this morass: to understand the debates, to be able to read and assess other people's statistical reports, and make appropriate choices when designing and analysing their own experiments, empirical studies, and other forms of quantitative data gathering.

KEYWORDS

statistics, human–computer interaction, quantitative data, evaluation, hypothesis testing, Bayesian statistics significance testing, p-hacking

Contents

Preface

Sometimes, it seems we are bombarded with numbers, from global warming to utility bills. In user research or academic studies, we may also encounter more formal statistics such as significance testing (all those p-values) or Bayesian methods; and graphs and tables, of course, are everywhere.

For those of us working with people, we know that numbers do not capture the complexities of social activity or the nuances of human feelings, which are often more appropriately explored through rich qualitative studies. Indeed, many researchers shun anything numerical as, at best, simplistic and, at worst, dehumanising.

However, the truth is that we all use statistics, both in our work and day-to-day lives. This may be obvious if you read an article with explicit statistics, but mostly the statistics we use are informal and implicit. If you eyeball a graph, table of results, or simple summary of survey responses, and it affects your opinions, you are making a statistical inference. If you interview a selection of people or conduct a user trial of new software and notice that most people mention a particular issue or have a particular problem, you are using statistics.

Below the surface, our brains constantly average and weigh odds and we may be subconsciously aware of statistical patterns in the world well before we explicitly recognise them. Statistics are everywhere and, consciously or unconsciously, we are all statisticians. The core question is how well we understand this.

This book is intended to fill the gap between the 'how to' knowledge in basic statistics books and a real understanding of what those statistics mean. It will help you make sense of the various alternative approaches presented in recent articles in HCI and wider scientific literature. In addition, the later chapters will present aspects of statistical 'craft' skills that are rarely considered in standard textbooks. Some of the book relates to more formal statistics, while other parts will be useful even if you are only eyeballing graphs or making qualitative judgements about data.

There are some excellent books on advanced statistical techniques within HCI: Robertson and Kaptein's collection *Modern Statistical Methods for HCI* [62] and Cairns' *Doing Better Statistics in Human–Computer Interaction* [9]. This book is intended to complement these, allowing you to follow statistical arguments without necessarily knowing how to perform each of the analyses yourself, and, if you are using more advanced techniques, to understand them more thoroughly.

This book arose from a course on "Understanding Statistics" at CHI 2017, which itself drew on earlier short courses and tutorials from 20 years before. The fundamentals of statistics changed little in those 20 years; indeed, I could and should have written this book then. However, there have been two main developments, which have intensified both the need and the timeliness. The first is the increased availability, usability, and power of statistical tools such as R. These make it so much easier to apply statistics but can also lead to a false sense of security when complex methods are applied without understanding their purpose, assumptions and limitations. The second change has been a growing publicity about the problems of badly applied statistics—the 'statistical crisis': topics that were once only discussed amongst professional statisticians are now a matter of intense debate on the pages of *Nature* and in the halls of CHI. Again, this awareness is a very positive step but comes with the danger that HCI researchers and UX practitioners may reach for new forms of statistics with even less understanding and greater potential for misuse. Even worse, the fear of doing it wrong may lead some to avoid using statistics where appropriate or excuse abandoning it entirely.

We are in a world where big data rules, and nowhere more than in HCI where A–B testing and similar analysis of fine-grained logging means that automated analysis appears to be overtaking design expertise. To make sense of big data as well as the results of smaller laboratory experiments, surveys or field studies, it is essential that we are able to make sense of the statistics necessary to interpret quantitative data and to understand the limitations of numbers and how quantitative and qualitative methods can work together.

By the end of the book, you should have a richer understanding of: the nature of random phenomena and different kinds of uncertainty; the different options for analysing data and their strengths and weaknesses; ways to design studies and experiments to increase 'power'—the likelihood of successfully uncovering real effects; and the pitfalls to avoid and issues to consider when dealing with empirical data. I hope that you will be better equipped to understand reports, data, and academic papers that use statistical techniques and to critically assess the validity of their results and how they may apply to your own practice or research. Most importantly, you will be better placed to design studies that efficiently use available resources and appropriately, effectively, and reliably analyse the results.

INTENDED READERSHIP

This book is intended for both experienced researchers and students who have already engaged, or intend to engage, in quantitative analysis of empirical data or other forms of statistical analysis. It will also be of value to practitioners using quantitative evaluation. There will be occasional formulae, but the focus of the book is on conceptual understanding, not mathematical skills.

Alan Dix
April 2020

Acknowledgments

First, I would like to thank Fiona, my wife, for her ongoing support and for reading this manuscript with her customary detail, not least by highlighting my continual tendency to write 'it' and 'this' when it is not at all clear what they refer to. Thanks also to the reviewers whose constructive comments led to quite substantial changes to the structure of this book, attendees at various tutorials and courses over the years who have given feedback on earlier versions of this material—including Ben for pointing out various errors (including one very embarrassing one) in a late draft. The photo of me on the cover was taken by Daniel Parry, who managed to fit me in at short notice just before the country shut down due to COVID-19. Many thanks, of course, to all the staff at Morgan & Claypool, especially Diane, Tondo, and Christine and I'm sure many others who I don't know by name but have contributed in many ways to ensuring this book is of the highest quality.

Finally, writing this under coronavirus lockdown, the importance of understanding quantitative data is reinforced. I would like to dedicate this book to the frontline workers across the world during this critical time; in the UK, especially the staff of the NHS, but also all those providing essential services—from pharmacists and workers in care homes, to supermarket checkout assistants and parcel deliverers. Looking at the UK income distribution in Section 4.13, it is sobering to think that many of those who are putting their health and lives on the line will have incomes at the lowest end of these graphs. Behind every number is a human life. We can either use statistics to distance ourselves from the harsh reality of life or as a window to expose the neglected and overlooked. I hope that this book can help you achieve the latter.

Alan Dix
April 2020

CHAPTER 1

Introduction

In this introductory chapter we consider:

- the nature of human cognition, which makes it hard to understand probability, and hence why we need formal statistics;

- whether you need to worry about statistics at all;

- the way statistics operates to offer us insight into the complexities of the world; and

- the different phases in research and software development and where different forms of qualitative and quantitative analysis are appropriate.

1.1   WHY ARE PROBABILITY AND STATISTICS SO HARD?

Do you find probability and statistics hard? If so, don't worry, it's not just you; it's basic human psychology.

We have two systems of thought[1]: (i) subconscious reactions that are based on semi-probabilistic associations, and (ii) conscious thinking that likes to have one model of the world and is really bad at probability. This is why we need to use mathematics and other explicit techniques to help us deal with probabilities. Furthermore, statistics needs both this mathematics of probability and an appreciation of what it means in the real world. Understanding this means you don't have to feel bad about finding stats hard, and also helps to suggest ways to make it easier.

1.1.1   IN TWO MINDS

Skinner's famous experiments with pigeons (Fig. 1.1) showed how certain kinds of learning could be studied in terms of associations between stimuli and rewards. If you present a reward enough times with the behaviour you want, the pigeon will learn to do it even when the original reward no longer happens. The learning is semi-probabilistic in the sense that if rewards are more common the learning is faster, or if rewards and penalties both happen at different frequencies, then you get a level of trade-off in the learning. At a cognitive level one can think of strengths of association being built up with rewards strengthening them and penalties inhibiting them.

---

[1]For more extensive discussion of these issues see Kahneman's *Thinking, Fast and Slow* [43] or Gladwell's *Blink* [31].

Figure 1.1: Pigeon about to tap for food (source: `https://archive.org/details/controll`
`ingbehaviorthroughreinforcement`).

This kind of learning is not quite a weighted sum of past experience: for example, negative experiences typically count more than positive ones, and once a pattern is established it takes a lot to shift it. However, it is not so far from a probability estimate. We humans share these subconscious learning processes with other animals. They are powerful and lead to very rapid reactions, but need very large numbers of exposures to similar situations to establish memories.

Of course we are not just our subconscious! In addition, we have conscious thinking and reasoning, which enable us to learn from a single experience. Retrospectively we are able to retrieve a relevant past experience, compare it to what we are encountering now, and work out what to do based on it. This is very powerful, but unlike our more unconscious sea of overlapping memories and associations, our conscious mind is linear and is normally locked into a single model of the world. Because of that single model, this form of thinking is not so good at intuitively grasping probabilities, as is repeatedly evidenced by gambling behaviour and more broadly our assessment of risk.

One experiment used four packs of cards with different penalties and rewards to see how quickly people could assess the difference [5]. The experiment included some patients with prefrontal brain damage, but we'll just consider the non-patients. The subjects could choose cards from the different packs. Each pack had an initial reward attached to it, but when they turned over a card it might also have a penalty, "sorry, you've lost $500." Some of the packs, those with the higher initial per-card reward, had more penalties, and the other packs had a better balance of rewards. After playing for a while most subjects realised that the packs were different and could tell which were better. The subjects were also wired up to a skin conductivity sensor as used in a lie detector. Well before they were able to say that some of the card packs were worse than the others, they showed a response on the sensor when they were about to turn over a card from the disadvantageous pack—that is subconsciously they knew it was likely to be a bad card.

Because our *conscious* mind is not naturally good at dealing with probabilities we need to use the tool of mathematics to enable us to reason explicitly about them. For example, if the subjects in the experiment had kept a tally of good and bad cards, they would have seen, *in the numbers*, which packs were better.

1.1.2 MATHS AND MORE

Some years ago, when I was first teaching statistics, I remember learning that statistics education was known to be particularly difficult. This is in part because it requires a combination of maths and real-world thinking.

In statistics we use the explicit tallying of data and mathematical reasoning about probabilities to let us do quite complex reasoning from effects (measurements) back to causes (the real word phenomena that are being measured). So you do need to feel reasonably comfortable with this mathematics. However, even if you are a whizz at maths, if you can't relate this back to understanding about the real world, you are also stuck. It is a bit like the applied maths problems where people get so lost in the maths that they forget the units: "the answer is 42"—but 42 what? 42 degrees, 42 metres, or 42 bananas?

On the whole, those who are good at mathematics are not always good at relating their thinking back to the real world, and those of a more practical disposition are not always best at maths—no wonder statistics is hard!

However, knowing this we can try to make things better.

It is likely that the majority of readers of this book will have a stronger sense of the practical issues, so I will try to explain some of the concepts that are necessary, without getting deep into the mathematics of how they are calculated—leave that to the computer!

1.2 DO YOU NEED STATS AT ALL?

The fact that you have opened this book suggests that you think you should learn something about statistics. However, maybe the majority of your work is qualitative, or you typically do small-scale studies and you wonder if it is sufficient to eyeball the raw data and make a judgement.

Sometimes no statistics are necessary. Perhaps you have performed a small user trial and one user makes an error; you look at the circumstances and think "of course lots of users will have the same problem." Your judgement is based purely on past experience and professional knowledge.

However, suppose you have performed a survey comparing two alternative systems and asked users which system they prefer. The results are shown in Fig. 1.2. It is clear that System A is far more popular than System B. Or is it?

Notice that the left hand scale has two notches, but no values. Let's suppose first that the notches are at 1000 and 2000: the results of surveying 3000 people. This is obviously a clear result. However, if instead the notches were at 1 and 2, representing a survey of 3 users, you

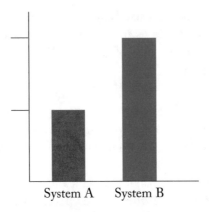

Figure 1.2: User preferences comparing two systems.

might not be so confident in the results. As you eyeball the data, you are performing some informal statistics.

What if it were 10 to 20, or 5 to 10? How clear a result would that be? The job of statistics is precisely to help you with judgements such as these.

1.3   THE JOB OF STATISTICS – FROM THE REAL WORLD TO MEASUREMENT AND BACK AGAIN

If you want to use statistics you will need to learn about t-tests and p-values, perhaps Bayesian statistics or Normal distributions, maybe a stats package such as SPSS or R. But why do this at all? What does statistics actually achieve?

Fundamentally, statistics is about trying to learn dependable things about the real world based on measurements of it.

However, what we mean by 'real' is itself a little complicated, from the actual users you have tested to the hypothetical idea of a 'typical user' of your system.

1.3.1   THE 'REAL' WORLD

We'll start with the real world, but what is that?

the sample First of all, there is the actual data you have: results from an experiment, responses from a survey, or log data from a deployed application. This is the real world. The user you tested at 3 PM on a rainy day in March, after a slightly overfilling lunch, did make precisely 3 errors and finished the task in 17 minutes and 23 seconds. However, while this measured data is real, it is typically not what you wanted to know. Would the same user on a different day, under different conditions, have made the same errors? What about other users?

the population Another idea of 'real' is when there is a larger group of people you want to know about, say all the employees in your company, or all users of product A. This larger group is often referred to as the population. What would be the average (and variation in) error rate if all of them sat down and used the software you are testing? Or, as a more concrete kind of measurement, what is their average height? You might take a sample of 20 people and find their average height, but you are using this to make an estimate about your population as a whole.

the ideal However, while this idea of the actual population is very concrete, often the 'real' world you are interested in is slightly more nebulous. Consider the current users of product A. You are interested in the error rate not only if they try your new software today, but if they do so multiple times over a period—that is, a sort of 'typical' error rate when each uses the software.

Furthermore, it is not so much the actual set of current users (not that you don't care about them), but rather the typical user, especially for a new piece of software where you have no current users yet. Similarly, when you toss a coin you have an idea of the behaviour of a fair coin, which is not simply the complete collection of every coin in circulation. Even when you have tossed the coin, you can still think about the different ways it *could* have fallen, somehow reasoning about all possible pasts and presents for an unrepeatable event.

the theoretical Finally, this hypothetical 'real' event may be represented mathematically as a theoretical distribution such as the Normal distribution (for heights) or Binomial distribution (for coin tosses).

In practice, you rarely need to voice these things explicitly, but occasionally you do need to think carefully about it. If you have done a series of consistent blood tests you may know something very important about a particular individual, but not patients in general. If you are analysing big data you may know something very precise about your current users, and how they behave given a particular social context and particular algorithms in your system, but not necessarily about potential users and how they may behave if your algorithms and environment change.

1.3.2   THERE AND BACK AGAIN

Once you have clarity about the 'real' world that you want to investigate, the job of statistics also becomes more clear. You have taken measurements, often of some sample of people and situations, and you want to use the measurements to understand the real world (Fig. 1.3).

For example, given a sample of heights of 20 randomly chosen people from your organisation, what can you infer about the heights of everyone? Given the error rates of 20 people on an artificial task in a lab, what can you tell about the behaviour of a typical user in their everyday situation? Given the complete past history of ten million users of a website, what does this tell us about their future behaviour or the behaviour of a new user to the site?

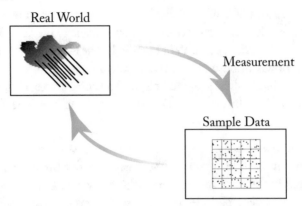

Figure 1.3: The job of statistics—moving from data about the real world back to knowledge about the real world.

1.3.3   NOISE AND RANDOMNESS

If all the measurements we had were deterministic, we would not need statistics. For example, an ultrasonic range finder sends a pulse of sound, measures how long it takes to return, then multiplies the time by the speed of sound, divides by two, and gives you a readout.

In the case of the sample of 20 people we can measure each of their heights relatively accurately, but maybe even this has some inaccuracy, so each measurement has some 'noise.' More critical is that they are randomly chosen from the far larger population of employees. In this and many similar situations, there is a degree of randomness in the measurements on which we base our decision making.

Just as with 'real,' 'random' is not so straightforward.

Some would argue that everything is pre-determined from its causes, with the possible exception of quantum mechanics, and even then only in some interpretations. However, in reality, when we toss a coin or roll a die, we treat these as probabilistic phenomena.

fundamentally random This is predominantly quantum-level processes such as the decay of radionuclides. These are used for some of the most critical random number generators.

complex processes When we toss a coin, the high speed of the spinning coin, coupled with the airflows around it as it falls, means that its path is so complex that it is effectively random. In the digital world, random number generators are often seeded by measuring a large number of system parameters, each in principle deterministic, but so complex and varied that they are effectively unpredictable.

past random events Imagine you have tossed a coin, and your colleague has taken a quick peek,[2] but you have not yet looked at it. What is the probability it is a head? Instinctively, you

---

[2]To avoid Schrödinger's cat type arguments.

would probably say "1 in 2." Clearly, it is already completely determined, but in *your state of knowledge* it is still effectively random.

uncontrolled factors As you go round measuring the heights of the people, perhaps tiny air movements subtly affect your ultrasonic height measurement. Or if you subsequently ask the people to perform a website navigation task, perhaps some have better web skills than others, or better spatial ability. Sometimes we can measure such effects, but often we have to treat them as effectively random.

Note that most people would regard the first two of these as 'really' random, or we could call them ontologically random—random in their actual state of being. In contrast the latter two are epistemologically random—random in your state of knowledge. In practice, we often treat all these similarly.

A more important set of distinctions that are of practical use are as follows:

persistence In some cases the random effect is in some way persistent (such as the skill or height of the person), but in other cases it is different for every measurement (like the air movements). This is important as the former may be measurable themselves, or in some circumstances can be cancelled out.

probability With the coin or die, we have an idea of the relative likelihood of each outcome, that is we can assign probabilities, such as 1/6 for the die rolling a '3'. However, some things are fundamentally unknown, such as trillionth digit of π; all we know is that it is one of the ten digits 0–9.

uniformity For the probabilistic phenomena, some are uniform: the chances of heads and tail are pretty much equal, as are the chances of landing on each of the six faces of a die. However, others are spread unevenly, such as the level of skill or height of a random employee. For the latter, we often need to be able to know or measure the shape of this unevenness (its distribution).

In order for statistics to be useful, the phenomena we deal with need to have some probability attached to them, but this does not need to be uniform, indeed probability distributions (see Chapter 4) capture precisely this non-uniformity. Philosophically, there are many ways we can think about these probabilities:

frequentist This is the most down-to-earth interpretation. When you say the chance of a coin landing heads is 50:50, you mean that if you keep on tossing the coin again and again and again, on average, after many many tosses, the ratio of heads to tails will be about 50:50. In the case of an unrepeatable phenomenon, such as the already tossed coin, this can be interpreted as "if I reset the world and re-ran it lots of times," though that, of course, is not quite so 'down to earth.'

idealist Plato saw the actual events of the world as mere reflections of deeper ideals. The toss of the actual coin in some ways is 'just' an example of an ideal coin toss. Even if you toss a coin five times in a row, and it happens to come up heads each time, you probably still believe that it is 'really' a 50:50 phenomenon.

formalist This is a pragmatic position: it doesn't matter what probability 'really' is, so long as it satisfies the right mathematical rules. In particular, Bayesian statistics encodes beliefs as 0–1 values, which satisfy the rules of probability (sometimes called plausibility or reasonable expectation [14, 40, 41]).

Often frequentist is used to refer to more traditional forms of statistics such as hypothesis testing (see Chapter 6), in contrast to Bayesian statistics (see Chapter 7), because the latter usually adopts the formalist approach, treating probability as belief. However, this is a misnomer as one can have frequentist interpretations of Bayesian methods and one can certainly apply formalism to traditional statistics. Personally, I tend to use frequentist language to explain phenomena, and formalism to do actual calculations ... but deep down I am an idealist!

We will explore and experiment further with randomness in the next chapter, but let us focus for the moment on the goal of working back from measurements to the real world. When the measurements include random effects, it is evident that answering questions about the real world requires a combination of probability and common sense—and that is precisely the job of statistics.

1.4   WHY ARE YOU DOING IT?

Are you doing empirical work because you are an academic addressing a research question, or a practitioner trying to design a better system? Is your work intended to test an existing hypothesis (validation) or to find out what you should be looking for (exploration)? Is it a one-off study, or part of a process (e.g., '5 users' for iterative development)?

These seem like obvious questions, but, in the midst of performing and analysing your study, it is surprisingly easy to lose track of your initial reasons for doing it. Indeed, it is common to read a research paper where the authors have performed evaluations that are more appropriate for user interface development, reporting issues such as wording on menus rather than addressing the principles that prompted their study.

This is partly because there are similarities between academic research and UX practice, both parallels in the empirical methods used and also parallels between the stages of each. Furthermore, your goals may shift—you might be in the midst of work to verify a prior research hypothesis, and then notice an anomaly in the data, which suggests a new phenomenon to study or a potential idea for a product.

We'll start out by looking at the processes of research and software development separately, and then explore the parallels. Being aware of the key stages of each helps you keep track of *why* you are doing a study and also *how* you should approach your work. In each we find stages

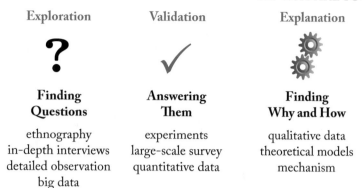

Figure 1.4: Research—different goals for empirical studies.

where different techniques are more or less appropriate: some need no statistics at all, instead qualitative methods such as ethnography are best; for some a 'gut' feeling for the numbers is sufficient, but no more; and some require formal statistical analysis.

1.4.1 EMPIRICAL RESEARCH

There are three main uses of empirical work during research, which often relate to the stages or goals of a research project (Fig. 1.4).

exploration This is principally about identifying the questions you want to ask. Techniques for exploration are often open-ended. They may be qualitative: ethnography, in-depth interviews, or detailed observation of behaviour whether in the lab or in the wild. However, this is also a stage that might involve (relatively) big data, for example, if you have deployed software with logging, or have conducted a large-scale, but open-ended, survey. Data analysis may then be used to uncover patterns, which may suggest research questions. Note, you may not need this as a stage of research if you began with an existing hypothesis, perhaps from previous phases of your own research, questions arising from other published work, or based on your own experiences.

validation This is predominantly about answering questions or verifying hypotheses. This is often the stage that involves most quantitative work: including experiments or large-scale surveys. This is also the stage that one most often publishes, especially in terms of statistical results, but that does not mean it is the most important. In order to validate, you must establish what you want to study (explorative) and what it means (explanation).

explanation While the validation phase confirms that an observation is true, or a behaviour is prevalent, this stage is about working out *why* it is true, and *how* it happens in detail. Work at this stage often returns to more qualitative or observational methods, but with a tighter

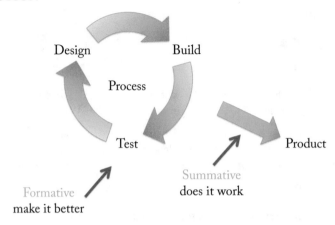

Figure 1.5: Iterative development process.

focus. However, it may also be more theory based, using existing models, or developing new ones in order to explain a phenomenon. Crucially it is about establishing mechanism, uncovering detailed step-by-step behaviours … a topic we shall return to later.

Of course these stages may often overlap, and data gathered for one purpose may turn out to be useful for another. For example, work intended for validation or explanation may reveal anomalous behaviours that lead to fresh questions and new hypotheses. However, it is important to know which goal you were *intending* to address, and, if you change, how and why you are looking at the data differently …and whether this matters.

1.4.2   SOFTWARE DEVELOPMENT

Figure 1.5 shows a typical iterative software development or user experience design cycle. Initial design activity leads to the making of some sort of demonstrable artefact. In the early stages this might be storyboards, or sketches, later wireframes or hi-res prototypes, or in the case of agile development an actual running system. This is then subjected to some form of testing or evaluation.

During this process we are used to two different kinds of evaluation point.

formative evaluation This is about making the system better. It is performed on the design artefacts (sketch, prototype, or experimental system) during the cycles of design–build–test. The form of this varies from expert evaluation to a large-scale user test. The primary purpose of formative evaluation is to uncover usability or experience problems for the next cycle.

summative evaluation This is about checking that the system works and is good enough. It is performed at the end of the software development process on a pre-release product. It

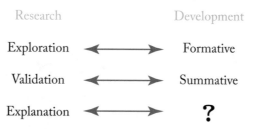

Figure 1.6: Parallels between academic research and iterative development.

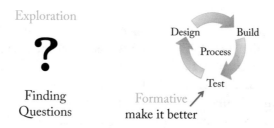

Figure 1.7: Parallel: exploration—formative evaluation.

may be related to contractual obligations: "95% of users will be able to use the product for purpose X after 20 minutes' training;" or may be comparative: "the new software outperforms competitor Y on both performance and user satisfaction." In less formal situations, it may simply be an assessment that enough work has been done based on the cumulative evidence from the formative stages.

In web applications, the boundaries can become a little less clear as changes and testing may happen on the live system as part of perpetual-beta releases or A–B testing.

1.4.3 PARALLELS

Although research and software development have different overall goals, we can see some obvious parallels between the two (Fig. 1.6). There are clear links between explorative research and formative evaluations, and between validation and summative evaluations. However, it is perhaps less immediately clear how explanatory research connects with development.

We will look at each in turn.

Exploration – formative

During the exploration stage of research or during formative evaluation of a product, you are interested in finding *any* interesting issue (Fig. 1.7). For research this is about something that you may then go on to study in depth and hope to publish papers about. In software development it is about finding usability problems to fix or identifying opportunities for improvements or

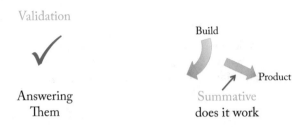

Figure 1.8: Parallel: validation—summative evaluation.

enhancements. It does not matter whether you have found the most important issue, or the most debilitating bug, so long as you have found sufficient for the next cycle of development.

Statistics are less important at this stage, but may help you establish priorities. If costs or time are short, you may need to decide which of the issues you have uncovered is most interesting to study further, or fix first. In practical usability, the challenge is not usually finding problems, nor even working out how to fix them; it is deciding which are worth fixing.

Validation – summative evaluation

In both validation in research and summative evaluation during development (Fig. 1.8), the focus is much more exhaustive: you want to find *all* problems and issues (though we hope that few remain during summative evaluation!).

The answers you need are definitive. You are not so much interested in new directions (though that may be an accidental outcome); instead, you are verifying that your precise hypothesis is true, or that the system works as intended. For this you may need statistical tests, whether traditional (p-value) or Bayesian (odds ratio).

You may also want figures: how good is it (e.g., "nine out of ten owners say their cats prefer …"), how prevalent is an issue (e.g., "95% of users successfully use the auto-grow feature"). For this the size of effects is important, so you may be more interested in confidence intervals, or pretty graphs with error bars on them.

As we noted earlier, in practical software development there may not be an explicit summative step, but the decision will be based on the ongoing cycles of formative assessment. This is of course a statistical assessment, however informal; perhaps you just note that the number and severity of problems found has decreased with each iteration. It may also be pragmatic: you've run out of time and are simply delivering the best product you have. However, if there is any form of external client, or if the product is likely to be business critical, there should be some form of quality assessment. The decision about whether to use formal statistical methods, eye-balling of graphs and data, or simple expert assessment will depend on many factors including the pragmatics of liability and available time.

Are five users enough?

One of the most well-known (and misunderstood) myths of interaction design is the idea that five users are enough.[a] I lose count of the number of times I have been asked about this, let alone seen variants of it quoted as a justification for study sizes in published papers.

The idea originated in a paper by Nielsen and Landaur [54], 25 years ago. However, that was crucially about formative evaluation during iterative evaluation. I emphasise, it was *neither* about summative evaluation, *nor* about sufficient numbers for statistics!

Nielsen and Landaur combined a simple theoretical model based on software bug detection with empirical data from a small number of substantial software projects to establish the optimum number of users to test *per iteration*.

Their notion of 'optimum' was based on cost—benefit analysis: each cycle of development costs a certain amount, each user test costs a certain amount. If you uncover too few user problems in each cycle you end up with many development cycles, which is expensive in terms of developer time. However, if you perform too many user tests you repeatedly find the same problems, thus wasting user-testing effort.

The optimum value depends on the *size and complexity* of the project, with the number far higher for more complex projects, where redevelopment cycles are more costly; the figure of five was a rough average based on the projects studied at the time. Nowadays, with better tool support, redevelopment cycles are far less expensive than any of the projects in the original study, and there are arguments that the optimal value may now even be just testing one user [50]—especially if it is obvious that the issues uncovered are ones that appear likely to be common. This idea of one-by-one testing has been embedded in the RITE method (Rapid Iterative Testing and Evaluation), which in addition advocates having various stakeholders heavily involved in very rapid cycles of testing and fixing [52, 53].

However, whether 1, 5, or 20 users, there will be more users on the next iteration—this is not about the total number of users tested during development. In particular, at later stages of development, when the most glaring problems have been fixed, it will become more important to ensure you have covered a sufficient range of the target user group.

For more on this see Jakob Nielsen's more recent and nuanced advice [55] and my own analyses of "Are five users enough?" [20].

[a]Indeed one of the reviewers of this book thought that the whole issue was so misleading that perhaps it shouldn't even be given the credibility of being mentioned.

Figure 1.9: Parallel: explanation.

Explanation

While validation establishes that a phenomenon occurs, *what* is true, explanation tries to work out *why* it happens and *how* it works (Fig. 1.9)—deep understanding.

As noted, this will often involve more qualitative work on small samples of people. However, it is also often best connected with quantitative studies of large samples. For example, you might have a small number of rich in-depth interviews, but match the participants against the demographics of large-scale surveys. If, say, a particular pattern of response is evident in the large study and your in-depth interviewee has a similar response, it is often a reasonable assumption that their reasons will be similar to the large sample. Of course, they could just be saying the same thing for completely different reasons, but often common sense or prior knowledge means that the reliability is evident. If you are uncertain of the reliability of the explanation, that could always drive targeted questions in a further round of large-scale surveys.

Similarly, if you have noticed a particular behaviour in logging data from a deployed experimental application, and a user has the same behaviour during a think aloud session or eye-tracking session, then it is reasonable to assume that their vocal deliberations and cognitive or perceptual behaviours may be similar to those of the users of the deployed application.

We noted that the parallel with software development was unclear; however, the last example starts to point toward a connection.

During the development process, user testing often reveals many minor problems. It iterates toward a good-enough solution, but rarely makes large-scale changes. Furthermore, at worst, the changes you perform at each cycle may create new problems. This is a common problem with software bugs where code becomes fragile, and with user interfaces, where each change in the interface creates further confusion, and may not even solve the problem that gave rise to it. After a while you may lose track of why each feature is there at all.

Rich understanding of the underlying human processes—perceptual, cognitive, social—can both ensure that 'bug fixes' actually solve the problem, and allow more *radical, but informed redesign* that may make whole rafts of problems simply disappear.

1.5   WHAT'S NEXT

The rest of this book is divided into three parts.

Wild and wide—concerning randomness and distributions. This part will help you get a 'gut feel' for random phenomena and some of the ways to describe and understand probabilities. In Chapter 2, we will explore this using a number of coin-tossing experiments, and then look at key concepts: in Chapter 3 bias, variability, and independence and in Chapter 4 probability distributions.

Doing it—if not p then what. This part is about being able to make sense of the statistics you see in articles and reports. After exploring the general issue of the job of statistics further in Chapter 5, Chapter 6 covers traditional statistics (hypothesis testing and confidence intervals), and Chapter 7 introduces Bayesian statistics. For each we will consider what they mean and, as importantly, misinterpretations. Chapter 8 describes some of the common issues and problems faced by all these statistical methods including the dangers of cherry picking and the benefits of simulation and empirical methods made possible by computation. Chapter 9 focuses on the differences and my own recommendations for best choice of methods.

Design and interpretation. The last part of this book is focused on the decisions you need to make as you design your own studies and experiments, and interpret the results. Chapter 10 is about increasing the statistical power of your studies, that is making it more likely you will spot real effects. Chapter 11 moves on to when you have results and want to make sense of them and present them to others; however, much of this advice is also relevant when you are reading the work of others. Finally, Chapter 12 reviews the current state of statistics within HCI and recent developments including adoption of new statistical methods and the analysis of big data.

PART I

Wild and Wide – Concerning Randomness and Distributions

CHAPTER 2

The unexpected wildness of random

How random is the world? We often underestimate just how wild random phenomena are—we expect to see patterns and reasons for what is sometimes entirely arbitrary.

By 'wild' here I mean that the behaviour of random phenomena is often far more chaotic than we expect. Perhaps because, barring the weather, so many aspects of life are controlled, we have become used to 'tame,' predictable phenomena. Crucially, this may lead to misinterpreting data, especially in graphs, either seeing patterns that are in fact pure randomness, or missing trends hidden by noise.

The mathematics of formal statistics attempts to see through this noise and give a clear view of robust properties of the underlying phenomenon. This chapter may help you see why you need to do this sometimes. However, we are also aiming to develop a 'gut' feeling for randomness, which is most important when you are simply eyeballing data, getting that first impression, to help you sort out the spurious from the serious and know when to reach for the formal stats.

2.1   EXPERIMENTS IN RANDOMNESS

Through a story and some exercises, I hope that you will get a better feel for how wild randomness is. We sometimes expect random things to end up close to their average behaviour, but we'll see that variability is often large.

When you have real data you have a combination of some real effect and random 'noise.' However, if you do some coin tossing experiments you can be sure that the coins you are dealing with are (near enough) fair—everything you see will be sheer randomness.

2.1.1   RAINFALL IN GHEISRA

We'll start with a story:

> In the far-off land of Gheisra there lies the Plain of Nali. For 100 miles in each direction it spreads, featureless and flat, no vegetation, no habitation; except, at its very centre, a pavement of 25 tiles of stone, each perfectly level with the others and with the surrounding land.
>
> The origins of this pavement are unknown—whether it was set there by some ancient race for its own purposes, or whether it was there from the beginning of the world.

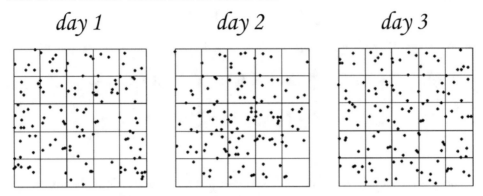

Figure 2.1: Three days in Gheisra—Which are mere chance and which are an omen?

> *Rain falls but rarely on that barren plain, but when clouds are seen gathering over the Plain of Nali, the monks of Gheisra journey on pilgrimage to this shrine of the ancients, to watch for the patterns of the raindrops on the tiles. Oftentimes the rain falls by chance, but sometimes the raindrops form patterns, giving omens of events afar off.*

Some of the patterns recorded by the monks are shown in Fig. 2.1. All of them at first glance seem quite random, but are they really? Do some have properties or tendencies that are not entirely like random rainfall? Which are mere chance, and which foretell great omens? *Before* reading on make your choices and record *why* you made your decision.

Before we reveal the true omens, you might like to know how you fare alongside three- and seven-year-olds.

When very young children are presented with this choice (with an appropriate story for their age) they give very mixed answers, but have a small tendency to think that distributions like Day 1 are real rainfall, whereas those like Day 3 are an omen.

In contrast, once children are older, seven or so, they are more consistent and tended to plump for Day 3 as the random rainfall.

Were you more like the three-year-old and thought Day 1 was random rainfall, or more like the seven-year-old and thought Day 1 was an omen and Day 3 random. Or perhaps you were like neither of them and thought Day 2 was true random rainfall.

Let's see who is right.

Day 1 When you looked at Day 1 you might have seen a slight diagonal tendency with the lower-right corner less dense than the upper-left. Or you may have noted the suspiciously collinear three dots in the second tile on the top row. However, this pattern, the preferred choice of the three-year-old, is in fact the random rainfall—or at least as random as a computer random number generator can manage! In true random phenomena you often do get gaps, dense spots, or apparent patterns, but this is just *pure chance*.

Day 2 In Day 2 you might have thought it looked a little clumped toward the middle. In fact, this is perfectly right, it is exactly the same tiles as in Day 1, but re-ordered so that the fuller tiles are toward the centre, and the part-empty ones to the edges. This is *an omen*!

Day 3 Finally, Day 3 is also *an omen*. This is the preferred choice of seven-year-olds to be random rainfalls and also, I have found, the preferred choice of 27-, 37-, and 47-year-olds. However, it is *too uniform*. The drops on each tile are distributed randomly within it, but there are precisely five drops on each tile. At some point during our early education we 'learn' (wrongly!) that random phenomena are uniform. Although this is nearly true when there are very large numbers involved (maybe 12,500 drops rather than 125), with smaller numbers the effects are far more chaotic than one might imagine.

2.1.2 TWO-HORSE RACES

Now for a different exercise, and this time you don't just have to choose, you have to do something.

Find a coin or, even better, if you have 20, get them. Toss the coins one by one and put the heads into one row and the tails into another. Keep on tossing until one line of coins has ten coins in it … you could even mark a finish line ten coins away from the start (like Fig. 2.2). If you only have one coin you'll have to toss it lots of times and keep tally.

If you are on your own repeat this several times, but if you are in a group, perhaps a class, do it fewer times and look at each other's coins as well as your own.

Before you start, think about what you expect to see, and only then do the coin tossing.

So what happened? Did you get a clear winner, or were they neck and neck? Is it what you expected to happen?

I had a go and did five races. In one case they were nearly neck-and-neck at 9 heads to 10 tails, but the other four races were all won by heads with some quite large margins: 10 to 7, 10 to 6, 10 to 5, and 10 to 4.

Often people are surprised because they are expecting a near neck-and-neck race every time. As the coins are all fair, they expect approximately equal numbers of heads and tails. However, just like the rainfall in Gheisra, it is very common to have one quite far ahead of the other.

You might think that because the probability of a head is a half, the number of heads will be near enough half. Indeed, this is the case if you average over lots and lots of tosses. However, with just 20 coins in a race, the variability is large.

The probability of getting an outright winner all heads or all tails is low, only about 1 in 500. However, the probability of getting a near wipe-out with 1 head and 10 tails or vice versa is around 1 in 50—in a large class one person is likely to have this.

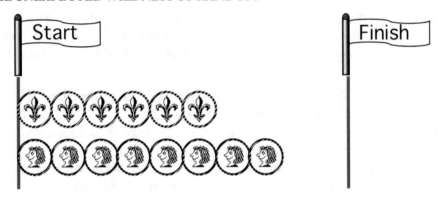

Figure 2.2: Two-horse races—Were yours neck-and-neck or was there a front runner?

2.1.3 LESSONS

I hope these two activities begin to give you some idea of the wild nature of random phenomena. We can see a few general lessons.

First, apparent patterns or differences may just be pure chance. For example, if you had found heads winning by 10 to 2, you might have thought this meant that your coin was in some way biased to heads. Or, you might have thought that the nearly straight line of three drops on Day 1 had to mean something. But random things are so wild that apparently systematic effects sometimes happen by chance.

Second, this wildness may lead to what appear to be 'bad values.' If you had got 10 tails and just 1 head, you might have thought "but coins are fair, so I must have done something wrong." Indeed, famous scientists have fallen for this fallacy!

Mendel's experiment on inheritance of sweet pea characteristics laid the foundations for modern genetics. However, his results are a little *too good*. If you cross-pollinate two plants, one of them pure bred to have a recessive characteristic (say R) and the other purely dominant (say D), in the first generation all the progeny have the dominant characteristic, but in fact possess precisely one recessive and one dominant gene (RD). In the second generation, interbreeding two of the first-generation RD plants is expected to have observable characteristics that are dominant and recessive in the ideal ratio 3:1. In Mendel's data the ratios are just a little *too close* to this figure. It seems likely that he rejected 'bad values,' assuming he had done something wrong, when in fact they were just the results of chance.

The same thing can happen in physics. In 1909, Robert Millikan and Harvey Fletcher ran an experiment to determine the charge of a single electron. The experiment (also known as the 'Millikan Can Experiment') found that charge came in discrete units and thus showed that each electron has an identical charge. To do this they created charged oil drops and suspended them using the electrostatic charge. The relationship between the electrical field needed and the size (and hence weight) of a drop enabled them to calculate the charge on each oil drop. These always came in multiples of a single value—the electron charge. There are always sources of error in any measurements and yet the reported charges are a little *too close* to multiples of the same number. Again, it looks like 'bad' results were ignored as some form of mistake during the setup of the experiment.

2.2   QUICK (AND DIRTY!) TIP

We often deal with survey or count data. This might come in public forms such as opinion poll data preceding an election, or from your own data when you email out a survey, or count kinds of errors in a user study.

So when you find that 27% of the users in your study had a problem, how confident do you feel in using this to estimate the level of prevalence amongst users in general? If you did a bigger study with more users would you be surprised if the figure you got was actually 17%, 37%, or 77%?

You can work out precise numbers for this, but I often use a simple rule of thumb method for doing a quick estimate.

for survey or other count data
do square root times two (ish)

We're going to deal with this by looking at three separate cases.

2.2.1   CASE 1 – SMALL PROPORTIONS

First, consider the case when the number you are dealing with is a comparatively small proportion of the overall sample. For example, assume you want to know about people's favourite colours. You do a survey of 1000 people and 10% say their favourite colour is blue. How reliable is this figure? If you had done a larger survey, would the answer still be close to 10% or could it be very different?

The simple rule is that the variation is 2x the square root number of people who chose blue.

To work this out, first calculate how many people the 10% represents. Given the sample was 1000, this is 100 people. The square root of 100 is 10, so 2x this is 20 people. You can be reasonably confident that the number of people choosing blue in your sample is within +/- 20 of the proportion you'd expect from the population as a whole. Dividing that +/-20 people by the 1000 sample, the % of people for whom blue is their favourite colour is likely to be within +/- 2% of the measured 10%.

2.2.2   CASE 2 – LARGE MAJORITY

The second case is when you have a large majority who have selected a particular option. For example, let's say in another survey, this time of 200 people, 85% said green was their favourite colour.

This time you still apply the "2x square root" rule, but instead focus on the smaller number, those who didn't choose green. The 15% who didn't choose green is 15% of 200, that is 30 people. The square root of 30 is about 5.5, so the expected variability is about +/-11, or in percentage terms about +/- 5%. That is, the real proportion over the population as a whole could be anywhere between 80% and 90%.

Notice how the variability of the proportion estimate from the sample increases as the sample size gets smaller.

2.2.3   CASE 3 – MIDDLING

Finally, if the numbers are near the middle, just take the square root, but this time multiply by 1.5.

For example, if you took a survey of 2000 people and 50% answered yes to a question, this represents 1000 people. The square root of 1000 is a bit over 30, and 1.5x this is around 50 people, so you expect a variation of about +/- 50 people, or about +/- 2.5%.

Opinion polls for elections often have samples of around 2000, so if the parties are within a few points of each other you really have no idea who will win.

2.2.4   WHY DOES THIS WORK?

For those who'd like to understand the detailed stats for this (skip if you don't!) …

These three cases are simplified forms of the precise mathematical formula for the variance of a Binomial distribution $np(1 - p)$, where n is the number in the sample and p the true population proportion for the thing you are measuring. When you are dealing with fairly small proportions the $1 - p$ term is close to 1, so the whole variance is close to np, that is the number with the given value. You then take the square root to give the standard deviation. The factor of 2 is because about 95% of measurements fall within 2 standard deviations. The reason this becomes 1.5 in the middle is that you can no longer treat $(1 - p)$ as nearly 1, and for $p = 0.5$, this makes things smaller by square root of 0.5, which is about 0.7. Two times 0.7 is (about) one and half (I did say quick and dirty!).

2.2.5   MORE IMPORTANT THAN THE MATH …

However, for survey data, or indeed any kind of data, these calculations of variability are in the end far less critical than ensuring that the sample really does adequately measure the thing you are after.

Figure 2.3: Monty Hall problem—Should you swap doors? (source: `https://en.wikipedia`
`.org/wiki/Monty_Hall_problem#/media/File:Monty_open_door.svg`.

Is it fair?—Has the way you have selected people made one outcome more likely. For example, if you do an election opinion poll of your Facebook friends, this may not be indicative of the country at large!

For surveys, has there been self-selection?—Maybe you asked a representative sample, but who actually answered? Often you get more responses from those who have strong feelings about the issue. For usability of software, this probably means those who have had a problem with it.

Have you phrased the question fairly?—For example, people are far more likely to answer "Yes" to a question, so if you ask "do you want to leave?" you might get 60% saying "yes" and 40% saying "no," but if you asked the question in the opposite way "do you want to stay?," you might still get 60% saying "yes."

We will discuss these kinds of issue in greater detail in Chapter 11.

2.3   PROBABILITY CAN BE HARD – FROM GOATS TO DNA

Simple techniques can help, but even mathematicians can get it wrong.

It would be nice if there was a magic bullet to make all of probability and statistics easy. I hope this book will help you make more sense of statistics, but there will always be difficult cases—our brains are just not built for complex probabilities. However, it may help to know that even experts can get it wrong!

We'll look now at two complex issues in probability that even mathematicians sometimes find hard: the Monty Hall problem and DNA evidence. We'll also see how a simple technique can help you tune your common sense for this kind of problem. This is *not* the magic bullet, but it may sometimes help.

2.3.1   THE MONTY HALL PROBLEM

There was a quiz show in the 1950s where the star prize was a car. After battling their way through previous rounds the winning contestant had one final challenge. There were three doors, behind one of which was the prize car, but behind each of the other two was a goat.

The contestant chose a door, but to increase the drama of the moment, the quizmaster did not immediately open the chosen door. Instead, they opened one of the others. The quizmaster, who knew which was the winning door, would always open a door with a goat behind. The contestant was then given the chance to change their mind. Imagine you are the contestant. What do you think you should do?

- Should you stick with the original choice?

- Should you change to the remaining unopened door?

- Or, doesn't it make any difference?

Although there is a correct answer, there are several apparently compelling arguments in either direction:

One argument is that, as there were originally three closed doors, the chance of the car being behind the door you chose first was 1 in 3, whereas now that there are only two closed doors to choose from, the chance of it being behind the one you didn't choose originally is 1 in 2, so you should change. However, the astute may have noticed that this is a slightly flawed probabilistic argument, as the probabilities don't add up to one.

A counter argument is that at the end there are two closed doors, so the chances are even as to which has the car behind it, and hence there is no advantage to changing.

An information theoretic argument is similar—the remaining closed doors hide the car equally before and after the other door has been opened: you have no more knowledge, so why change your mind?

Even mathematicians and statisticians can argue about this, and when they work it out by enumerating the cases, they do not always believe the answer. It is one of those cases where common sense simply does not help ... even for a mathematician!

Before revealing the correct answer, let's have a thought experiment.

2.3.2   TIP: MAKE THE NUMBERS EXTREME

Imagine if instead of three doors there were a million doors. Behind 999,999 doors are goats, but behind the one lucky door there is a car.

I am the quizmaster and ask you to choose a door. Let's say you choose door number 42. Now I now open 999,998 of the remaining doors, being careful to only open doors that hide goats. You are left with two doors, your original choice and the one door I have not opened. Do you want to change your mind?

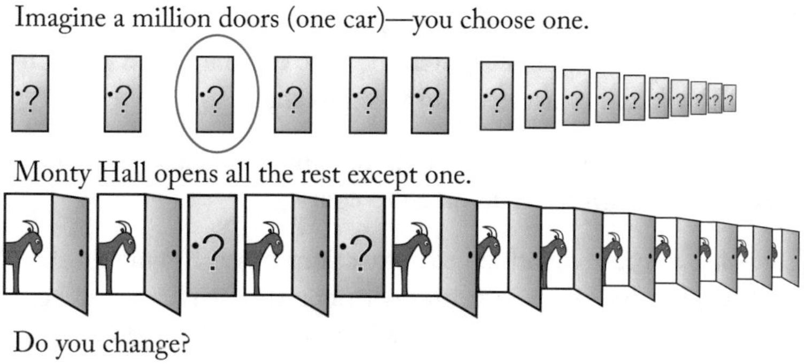

Imagine a million doors (one car)—you choose one.

Monty Hall opens all the rest except one.

Do you change?

Figure 2.4: Monty Hall with a million doors?

This time it is pretty obvious that you should change. There was virtually no chance of you having chosen the right door to start with, so it was almost certainly (999,999 out of a million) one of the others—I have helpfully discarded all the rest so the remaining door I didn't open is almost certainly the correct one.

It is as if, before I opened the 999,998 'goat' doors, I'd asked you, "do you think the car is precisely behind door 42, or *any* of the others?"

In fact, exactly the same reasoning holds for three doors. In that case there was a 2/3 chance that the car was behind one of the two doors you did not choose, and as the quizmaster I discarded one of those, the one that hid a goat. So it is twice as likely as your original choice that the car is behind the door I did not open. Regarding the information theoretic argument: the act of opening the goat door does add information because the quizmaster knows which door hides the car, and only opens a goat door. However, it still feels a bit like smoke and mirrors with three doors, even though the million-door version is obvious.

Using the extreme case helps tune your common sense, often allowing you to see flaws in mistaken arguments, or work out the true explanation. It is not an infallible heuristic (sometimes arguments do change with scale), but it is often helpful.

2.3.3   DNA EVIDENCE

The Monty Hall problem has always been a bit of fun, albeit disappointing if you were the contestant who got it wrong. However, there are similar kinds of problem where the outcomes are deadly serious. DNA evidence is just such an example. Although each person's DNA is almost unique, DNA testing is imperfect and has the possibility of error.

Suppose there has been a murder, and remains of DNA have been found on the scene. The lab DNA matching has an accuracy of one in 100,000.

Imagine two scenarios.

Case 1: Shortly prior to the body being found, the victim had been known to have had a violent argument with a friend. The police match the DNA of the friend with DNA found at the murder scene. The friend is arrested and taken to court.

Case 2: The police look up the DNA in the national DNA database and find a positive match. The matched person is arrested and taken to court.

Similar cases have occurred and led to convictions based heavily on the DNA evidence. However, while in case 1 the DNA is strong corroborating evidence, in case 2 it is not. Yet courts, guided by 'expert' witnesses, have not understood the distinction and convicted people in situations like case 2. Belatedly, the problem has been recognised and in the UK there have been a number of appeals where longstanding cases have been overturned, sadly not before people have spent considerable periods behind bars for crimes they did not commit. One can only hope that similar evidence has not been crucial in jurisdictions with a death penalty.

If you were the judge or jury in such a case would the difference be obvious to you?

If not, we can use a similar trick to the one we used in the Monty Hall problem. There, we made the numbers a lot bigger; here we will make the numbers less extreme. Instead of a 1 in 100,000 chance of a false DNA match, let's make it 1 in 100. While this is still useful, though not overwhelming, corroborative evidence in case 1, it is pretty obvious that if there are more than a few hundred people in the police database, then you are bound to find a match.

It is as if a red Fiat Uno had been spotted outside the victim's house. If the friend's car was a red Fiat Uno it would be good additional circumstantial evidence, but simply arresting any red Fiat Uno owner would clearly be silly.

If we return to the original 1 in 100,000 figure for a DNA match, it is the same. If there are more than a few hundred thousand people in the database then you are almost bound to find a match. This might be a way to find people you might investigate by looking for other evidence, indeed that's the way several cold cases have been solved over recent years, but the DNA evidence would not *in itself* be strong.

In summary, some diverting puzzles and also some very serious problems involving probability can be very hard to understand. Our common sense is not well tuned to probability. Even trained mathematicians can get confused, which is one of the reasons we turn to formulae and calculations. However, we saw that changing the scale of numbers in a problem can sometimes help your common sense to understand them.

CHAPTER 3

Properties of randomness

We've seen how wild random phenomena can be; however, this does not mean they cannot be understood and at least partially tamed.

3.1 BIAS AND VARIABILITY

When you take a measurement, whether it is the time for someone to complete a task using some software, or a preferred way of doing something, you are using that measurement to find out something about the 'real' world—the average time for completion, or the overall level of preference amongst your users.

Two of the core things you need to know about are bias (is it a fair estimate of the real value) and variability (how likely is it to be close to the real value). Are your results fair and are they reliable?

3.1.1 BIAS

The word 'bias' in statistics has a precise meaning, but it is very close to its day-to-day meaning. Bias is about systematic effects that skew your results in one way or another. In particular, if you use your measurements to predict some real-world effect, is that effect likely to over- or under-estimate the true value? In other words, is it a *fair* estimate.

Say you take 20 users, and measure their average time to complete some task. You then use that as an estimate of the 'true' value, the average time to completion of all your users. Your particular estimate may be low or high (as we saw with the coin tossing experiments). However, if you repeated that experiment very many times would the average of your estimates end up being the true average?

If the complete user base were employees of a large company, and the company forced them to engage in your study, you could randomly select your 20 users, and in that case, yes, the estimate based on the users would be unbiased.[1]

However, imagine you are interested in the popularity of Ariana Grande and issued a survey on a social network as a way to determine this. The effects would be very different depending on whether you chose to use LinkedIn or TikTok. No matter how randomly you select users from LinkedIn, they are probably not representative of the population as a whole, so you would end up with a biased estimate of Grande's popularity.

---

[1] Assuming they behaved as normal in the test and weren't annoyed at being told to be 'volunteers.'

Crucially, the typical way to improve an estimate in statistics is to take a bigger sample: more users, more tasks, more tests on each user. Unfortunately, bias usually persists no matter the sample size.[2]

However, the good news is that sometimes it is possible to model bias and correct for it. For example, you might ask questions about age or other demographics and then use known population demographics to add weight to groups under-represented in your sample ... although I doubt this would work for the Ariana Grande example: if there are 15-year-old members of LinkedIn, they are unlikely to be typical 15-year-olds!

If you have done an introductory statistics course you might have wondered about the '$n - 1$' that occurs in calculations of standard deviation or variance. In fact, this is precisely a correction for bias: the raw standard deviation of a sample slightly underestimates the real standard deviation of the overall population. This is pretty obvious in the case $n = 1$. Imagine picking someone random from the street and measuring their height. Using that height as an average height for everyone would be pretty unreliable, but it is unbiased. However, the standard deviation of that sample of 1 is zero. The sample is one number, there is no spread. This underestimation is less clear for samples of 2 or more, but it does persist in larger samples. Happily, in this case you can accurately model the underestimation; the use of $n - 1$ rather than n in the formulae for estimated standard deviation and variance exactly corrects for the underestimation.

3.1.2   BIAS VS. VARIABILITY

If you toss ten coins, there is only a 1 in 500 chance of getting either all heads or all tails, and about a 1 in 50 chance of getting only 1 head or 1 tail, the really extreme values are relatively unlikely. However, there is about a 1 in 10 chance of getting either just 2 heads or 2 tails. If you kept tossing the coins again and again, the times you got 2 heads and 8 tails would approximately balance the opposite and overall you would find that the average proportion of heads and tails would come out 50:50.

That is to say, the proportion you estimate by tossing just ten coins has a high variability, but is unbiased. It is a *poor estimate of the right thing.*

Often the answer is simply to take a larger sample—toss 100 coins or 1000 coins, not just ten. Indeed, when looking for infrequent events, physicists may leave equipment running for months on end, taking thousands of samples per second. You can sample yourself out of high variability!

Think now about studies with real users—if tossing ten coins can lead to such high variability, what about those measurements on ten users?

Often there may be time, cost, and practicality limits on how many users you can involve, so there are times when you can't just have more users. Chapter 10 on 'gaining power' includes

---

[2]Actually, there are some forms of bias that do go away with large samples, called asymptotically unbiased estimators, but this does not apply in the cases where the way you choose your sample has created an unrepresentative sample, or the way you have set up your study favours one outcome.

strategies to reduce variability and hence obtain more traction from the users and time you do have available.

In contrast, let's imagine you have performed a random survey of 10,000 LinkedIn users and obtained data on their attitudes to Ariana Grande. Let's say you found 5% liked Ariana Grande's music. Remembering the quick and dirty rule,[3] the variability on this figure is about +/- 0.5%. If you repeated the survey, you would be likely to get a similar answer. That is you have a very reliable estimate of her popularity amongst all LinkedIn users, but if you are interested in overall popularity, is this any use? You have a *good estimate of the wrong thing*.

As we've discussed you cannot simply sample your way out of this situation. If your process is biased it is likely to stay so. In this case you have two main options. You may try to eliminate the bias—maybe sample over a wide range of social networks that between them offer a more representative view of society as a whole. Alternatively, you might try to model the bias, and correct for it.

In summary, we have:

bias – a good estimate of the wrong thing

variability – a poor estimate of the right thing

On the whole, high variability is a problem but there are relatively straightforward strategies for dealing with it. Bias is your real enemy!

3.2   INDEPENDENCE AND NON-INDEPENDENCE

Independence is another key term in statistics. We will see several different kinds of independence, but in general it is about whether one measurement or factor gives information about another.

Non-independence may increase variability, lead to misattribution of effects, or even suggest completely the wrong effect.

Simpson's Paradox (discussed later in this chapter) is an example of the latter where, for example, you might see year-on-year improvement in the performance of each kind of student you teach and yet the university tells you that you are doing worse!

Imagine you have tossed a coin 10 times and it has come up heads each time. You know it is a fair coin, not a trick one. What is the probability it will be a tail next?

Of course, the answer is 50:50, but we often have a gut feeling that it should be more likely to be a tail to even things out. This is the uniformity fallacy that leads people to choose the pattern with uniformly dispersed drops in the Gheisra story in Chapter 2. It is exactly the same feeling that a gambler has when they put in a big bet after a losing streak, "surely my luck must change."

---

[3]5% of 10,000 represents 500 users. The square root of 500 is around 22, twice that a bit under 50, so our estimate of variability is 500+/-50, or, as a percentage of users, 5% +/- 0.5%.

In fact with the coin tosses, each is independent: there is no relationship between one coin toss and the next. However, there can be circumstances (for example looking out of the window to see it is raining), where successive measurements are not independent. This is the first of three kinds of independence we will look at:

- measurements,

- factor effects, and

- sample composition.

Each of these has slightly different causes and effects. In general, the main effect of non-independence is to increase variability of measures such as the average; however, sometimes it can also induce bias. Critically, if one is unaware of the issues it is easy to make false inferences: I have looked out of the window 100 times and it was raining each time, should I therefore conclude that it is always raining?

Paradoxically, in this example the non-independence will *decrease the variability within the sample* as each reading is likely to be similar; however, it *increases the variability between samples*. If you take 100 readings of the weather on one day and I take 100 on another, our estimates of the typical weather are likely to be quite different; however, if we had each taken our 100 readings over many different days, our estimates would be more likely to be similar. This is a double whammy: your estimate of the variability of your estimate is low, but its actual variability is high!

3.2.1 INDEPENDENCE OF MEASUREMENTS

We have already seen an example where successive measurements are independent (coin tosses) and one where they are not (looking out at the weather). In the latter case, if it is raining now it is likely still to be raining if I look again in 2 min; the second observation adds little information.

Many statistical tests assume that measurements are independent and need some sort of correction to be applied or care in interpreting results when this is not the case. However, there are a number of ways in which measurements may be related to one another.

order effects—This is one of the most common in experiments with users. A 'measurement' in user testing involves the user doing something, perhaps using a particular interface for ten minutes. You then ask the same user to try a different interface and compare the two. There are advantages to having the same user perform on different systems (reduces the effect of individual differences); however, there are also potential problems.

You may get positive learning effects: the user is better at the second interface because they have already got used to the general ideas of the application in the first. Alternatively, there may be interference effects: the user does less well in the second interface because they have got used to the detailed way things were done in the first.

One way this can be partially ameliorated is to alternate the order. Half the users see system A first, followed by system B; the other half see B followed by A. You may even do lots of swaps in the hope that the later ones have fewer order effects: ABABABABAB for some users and BABABABABA for others.

These techniques work best if any order effects are symmetric. If, for example, there is a positive learning effect between A and B, but a negative interference effect between B and A, alternating the order does not help! Typically, you cannot tell this from the raw data, although comments made during talk-aloud or post study interviews can help. In the end you often have to make a professional judgment based on experience as to whether you believe this kind of asymmetry is likely, or indeed if order effects happen at all.

context or **'day' effects**—Successively looking out of the window does not give a good estimate of the overall weather in the area because it is effectively about the particular weather at a particular location and nearly the same time. However, the weather is not immaterial to user testing, especially user experience evaluation, because bad weather often affects people's moods, and if people are less happy walking in to your study they are likely to perform less well and record lower satisfaction! More generally, you need to be alert for any element of the *context* that might affect your study.

If you are performing a controlled experiment, you probably try to follow a strict protocol, but there may be slight differences in the way you do things that push the experiment in one direction or another.

Some years ago I was working on hydraulic sprays, as used to deliver pesticides or herbicides on a farm. We had a laser-based drop sizing machine and I ran a series of experiments varying factors such as water temperature and surfactants added to the spray fluid, in order to ascertain whether these had any effect on the size of drops produced. The experiments were conducted in a sealed laboratory and were carefully controlled. When we analysed the results there were some odd effects that did not seem to make sense. After puzzling over this for some while one of my colleagues remembered that the experiments had occurred over two days and suggested we add a 'day effect' to the analysis. This seemed ridiculous at first, given the controlled nature of the experiment, but we re-ran the analysis 'just in case.' Sure enough this 'day effect' came out as a major factor and once it was included all the odd effects disappeared.

Now this was a physical system and we had tried to control the situation as well as possible, and yet still there was something, we never worked out what, that was different between the two days. Now think about a user test! You cannot predict every odd effect, but do make sure you mix your conditions as much as possible so that they are 'balanced' with respect to other factors. For example, if you are doing two sessions of experimentation try to have a mix of two systems you are comparing in each session (I know this is not always possible).

experimenter effects—A particular example of a contextual factor that may affect users' performance and attitude is you! You may have prepared a script so that you greet each user the same and present the tasks they have to do in the same way, but if you have had a bad day your mood may well come through.

Using pre-recorded or textual instructions can help, but it would be rude not to at least say "hello" when users come in, and often you want to set them at ease, so more personal contact is needed. As with other kinds of context effect, anything that can help balance out these effects is helpful. It may take a lot of effort to set up different testing systems, so you have to have a long run of testing one system and then a long run of another, but if this is the case you might consider one day testing system A in the morning and system B in the afternoon and then another day doing the opposite. If you do this, then, even if you have an off day, you affect both systems fairly. Similarly if you are a morning person, or get tired in the afternoons, this will again affect both fairly. You can never remove these effects, but you can be aware of them in order to mitigate them.

Crucially in all of these effects non-independence will *increase variability* of measures such as the mean.

3.2.2   INDEPENDENCE OF FACTOR EFFECTS

The second kind of independence is when there is some form of relationship or correlation between the various factors that you are measuring aspects of. For example, if you sampled LinkedIn and WhatsApp users and found that 5% of LinkedIn users were Ariana Grande fans compared with 50% of TikTok users, you might believe that there was something about LinkedIn that put people off Ariana Grande. However, of course, age will be a strong predictor of the Ariana Grande fandom and is also related to the choice of social network platform. In such a case social media use and age are called confounding variables.

As you can see it is easy for these effects to confuse causality.

A real example of this is that when you measure the death rate amongst patients in specialist hospitals it is often higher than in general hospitals. At first sight this makes it seem that patients do not get as good care in specialist hospitals, leading to lower safety, but in fact it is because patients admitted to specialist hospitals are usually more ill to start with.

This kind of effect can sometimes entirely reverse effects, leading to Simpson's Paradox.

Imagine you are teaching a course on UX design. You teach a mix of full-time and part-time students and you have noticed that the performance of both groups has been improving year on year. You pat yourself on the back, happy that you are clearly finding better ways to teach as you grow more experienced.

However, one day you get an email from the university teaching committee noting that your performance seems to be diminishing. According to the university your grades are dropping.

Who is right? In fact, you may *both* be.

The table on the right of Fig. 3.1 shows your *average full-time* student marks in 2015 and 2016 as 75% and 80%, an increase of 5%. In the same two years the *average part-time* student mark increased from 55% to 60%.

So, yes, both full-time and part-time students have improved their marks—you are right, the grades of each group are increasing

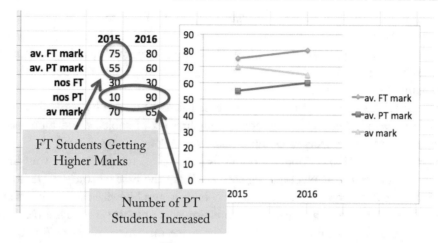

Figure 3.1: Who is right? You both are!

The university figures however show an *average overall* mark of 70% in 2015 dropping to 65% in 2016—they are right too, the average overall grade is falling.

Looking more closely, whilst there were 30 full-time students in both years the number of part-time students had increased from 10 in 2015 to 90 in 2016, maybe due to a university marketing drive or change in government funding patterns. Looking at the figures, the part-time students score substantially lower than the full-time students, not uncommon as part-time students are often juggling study with a job and may have been out of education for some years. The lower overall average that the university reports is entirely due to there being more low-scoring part-time students, not to poor teaching performance.

Although this seems like a contrived example, see [7] for a real example of Simpson's Paradox. Berkeley appeared to have gender bias in admissions because (at the time, 1973) women had only a 35% acceptance rate compared with 44% for men. However, deeper analysis found that in individual departments the bias was, if anything, slightly toward female candidates; the problem was that females tended to apply for more competitive courses with lower admission rates (possibly revealing discrimination earlier in the education process).

3.2.3   INDEPENDENCE OF SAMPLE COMPOSITION

Lastly, we look at how the way you obtain your sample may create lack of independence between your subjects.

This happens in two ways:

- internal—subjects related to each other; and

- external—subject choice related to topic.

internal non-independence—This is when subjects are likely to be similar to one another, but in no particular direction with regard to your question. A simple example of this would be if you did a survey of people waiting in the queue to enter a football match. The fact that they are next to each other in the queue might mean they all came off the same bus and so are more likely to support the same team.

Snowball samples are common in some areas. This is when you have an initial set of contacts, often friends or colleagues, use them as your first set of subjects and then ask them to suggest any of their own contacts who might take part in your survey.

Imagine you do this to get political opinions in the U.S., and you choose your first person to contact randomly from the electoral register. Let's say the first person is a Democrat. That person's friends are likely to share similar political beliefs, and likewise their contacts also. Your snowball sample will probably give you the impression that nearly everyone is a Democrat!

Typically this form of internal non-independence *increases real variability*, but *does not create bias*.

Imagine continuing to survey people in the football queue. Eventually you will get to a group of people from a different bus. After interviewing 500 people you might have thought you had pretty reliable statistics, but in fact that corresponds to about 10 buses, so its variability will be closer to a sample size of ten. Alternatively, if you sample 20 people, and colleagues also do samples of 20 each, some of you will think that nearly everyone supports one team, some will get data that suggest that nearly everyone supports the other team, but if you average your results you will get something that is unbiased.

A similar thing happens with the snowball sample. If you had instead started with a Republican you would probably have had a large sample, almost all of whom would have been Republican. If you repeated the process, each sample might be overwhelmingly one party or the other, but the long-term average of doing lots of snowball samples would be correct. In fact, just like doing a bigger sample on the football queue, if you continue the snowball process on the sample that started with the Democrat, you are likely to eventually find someone who is friends with a Republican and then come upon a big pocket of Republicans. However, again just like the football queue and the buses, while you might have surveyed hundreds of people, you may have only sampled a handful of pockets. The lack of internal independence means the effective sample size is a lot *smaller* than you think.

external non-independence—This is when the choice of subjects is actually connected with the topic being studied; for example, visiting an Apple Store and doing a survey about preferences between MacOS and Windows, or iPhone and Android. However, the effect may not be so immediately obvious; for example, using a mobile app-based survey on a topic which is likely to be age related.

The problem with this kind of non-independence is that it may lead to unintentional bias in your results. Unlike the football or snowball sample examples, surveying another 20 users in the Apple Store, and then another 20 and another 20, is not going to average out the fact that it is an Apple Store.

The crucial question to ask yourself is whether the way you have organised your sample is likely to be independent of the thing you want to measure.

The snowball sample example is clearly problematic for sampling political opinions, but may be acceptable for favourite colour or shoe size. The argument for this may be based on previous data, on pilot experiments, on professional knowledge, or common-sense reasoning. While there may be some cliques, such as members of a basketball team, with similar shoe size, I am making a judgement based on my own life experience that shared shoe size is not closely related to friendship, whereas shared political belief is.

The decision may not be so obvious, for example, if you run a Fitts' Law experiment and all the distant targets are coloured red and the close ones blue. Maybe this doesn't matter, or maybe there are odd peripheral vision reasons why it might skew the results. In this case, and assuming the colours are important, my first choice would be to include all conditions (including close red and distant blue targets) as well as the ones I'm interested in, or else run an alternative experiment or spend a lot of time checking out the vision literature.

Perhaps the most significant potential biasing effect is that we will almost always recruit subjects from the same society as ourselves. In particular, for university research this tends to mean undergraduate students. However, even the most basic cognitive traits in these subjects are not necessarily representative of the world at large [37], let alone more obviously culturally related attitudes. We will look at these issues again in Chapter 10 (Section 10.3).

3.3   PLAY!

The notions of bias and independence are central to many aspects of statistics, but can be hard to conceptualise, not least because in real life they are interwoven with so many other factors and of course the inherent randomness of the kinds of data statistics attempts to deal with.

Whilst tossing coins is a good way of getting a 'gut feel' for the randomness of unbiased and independent measurements, it does not help with these more complex phenomena.

To help you, the book's web resources include two web demonstrators that allow you to experiment with virtual coins. Because the coins are digital you can alter their properties, make them vary from 50:50 or make successive coin tosses not be independent of one another. Add positive correlation and see the long lines of heads or tails, or put in negative correlation and see the heads and tails swap on nearly every toss.

Links to the demonstrators and detailed documentation on how to use each can be found in the book's web resources. Incidentally, the demos were originally created in 1998: my very first interactive web pages. It is amazing how much you could do even with 1998 web technology!

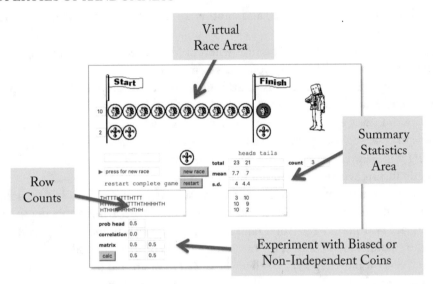

Figure 3.2: Virtual two-horse races.

3.3.1   VIRTUAL TWO-HORSE RACES

The first demonstrator (Fig. 3.2) automates the two-horse races that you have done by hand with real coins in the "unexpected wildness of random" exercises (see Chapter 2, Section 2.1.2). The application keeps track of the coin tosses, so that you can run multiple races and see how the vastly different individual races start to average out in the long term. More importantly, you can adjust the bias and independence of the virtual coins.

If you set the bias toward heads, you will start to see heads win most of the time, but tails may still win occasionally. Even if the coin is biased, the less likely outcome can still occur.

More interesting are the effects when you adjust the independence. You can set a positive correlation: the probability of a coin landing the same as the previous one is more likely than it changing. This is rather like the weather: if it is rainy today it is more likely to be rainy tomorrow; if it is sunny today then tomorrow is also likely to be sunny. You can also play with negative correlation when each virtual coin flip tends to be the opposite of the previous one—you then begin to see patterns of alternating heads and tails.

Play with the values to get a feel for how they affect the coin tossing. However, do remember to do plenty of coin tosses for each setting, otherwise all you will see is the randomness! Play first with quite extreme values, as the effects will be more evident.

3.3.2   MORE (VIRTUAL) COIN TOSSING

The second demonstrator (Fig. 3.3) looks very similar, but with no race track! It also allows you to create virtual coins with simulated bias and correlation between tosses. There are differences,

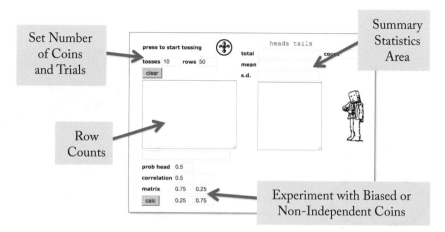

Figure 3.3: More (virtual) coin tossing—overview.

however: this does not do a two-horse race, but instead will toss a fixed number of coins, and then repeat. Also, you don't have to press the toss button for each coin toss, just once and it does as many as you ask. For example, you can ask it to toss 10 coins at a time, but then repeat the experiment 50 times. This helps you get a better grasp of the long-term averages and behaviour.

You can experiment with this yourself, but I've done a few experiments myself so you can see the results.

3.3.3 FAIR AND BIASED COINS

Figure 3.4 shows a set of tosses where the coin was set to be fair (prob head= 0.5) with completely independent tosses (correlation= 0)—that is just like a real coin (only faster).

You can see the first nine rows and first nine row counts in the left and right text areas. Note how the individual rows vary quite a lot, as we have seen in the physical coin tossing experiments. However, the average (over 50 sets of 10 coin tosses) is quite close to 50:50. The standard deviation is 1.8, but note that this is the standard deviation of the sample. Because this is a completely random coin toss, with well-understood probabilistic properties, it is possible to calculate the 'real' standard deviation—the value you would expect to see if you repeated this thousands and thousands of times. That value is the square root of 2.5, which is just under 1.6. The measured standard deviation is an *estimate* of the 'real' value, not the 'real' value itself, just as the measured proportion of heads has turned out at 0.49, not exactly a half. This estimate of the standard deviation itself varies a lot … indeed, estimates of variation are often very variable themselves (see Chapter 8, Section 8.3).

Figure 3.5 shows another set of tosses, this time with the probability of a head set to 0.25. That is a (virtual!) coin that falls heads about a quarter of the time, a bit like having a four-sided spinner with heads on one side and tails on the other three.

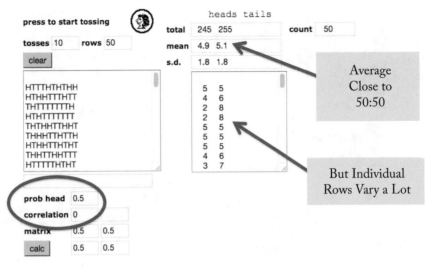

Figure 3.4: Fair coin (independent tosses).

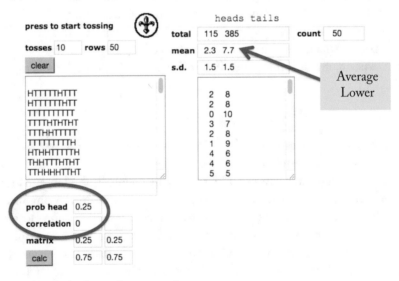

Figure 3.5: Biased coin (independent tosses).

The correlation has been set to zero still so that the tosses are independent.

You can see how the proportion of heads is now smaller, on average 2.3 heads to 7.7 tails in each run of 10 coins. Though this is not exactly 2.5, if you repeated the tosses it would sometimes be less, sometimes more. On average, over 1000s of tosses it would end up close to 2.5.

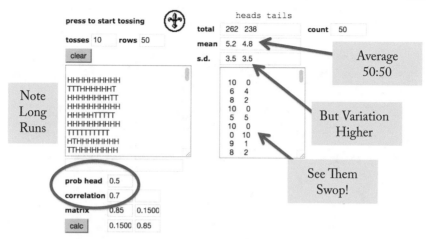

Figure 3.6: Positive correlation.

3.3.4 NO LONGER INDEPENDENT

Now we're going to play with very unreal non-independent coins.

In Fig. 3.6 the probability of being a head is set to 0.5, so it is a fair coin, but the correlation is positive (0.7), meaning heads are more likely to follow heads and vice versa.

If you look at the left-hand text area you can see the long runs of heads and tails. Sometimes they do alternate, but then stay the same for long periods.

Looking up to the summary statistics area the average numbers of heads and tails is near 50:50—the coin was fair—but the standard deviation is a lot higher than in the independent case. This is very evident if you look at the right-hand text area with the totals as they swing between extreme values much more than the independent coin did (even more than its quite wild randomness!).

If we put a negative value for the correlation (Fig. 3.6) we see the opposite effect. Now the rows of Hs and Ts alternate a lot of the time, far more than a normal coin.

The average is still close to 50:50, but this time the variation is lower and you can see this in the row totals, which are typically much closer to five heads and five tails than the ordinary coin.

Recall the gambler's fallacy that if a coin has fallen heads lots of times it is more likely to be a tail next. In some way this coin is a bit like that, effectively evening out the odds, hence the lower variation.

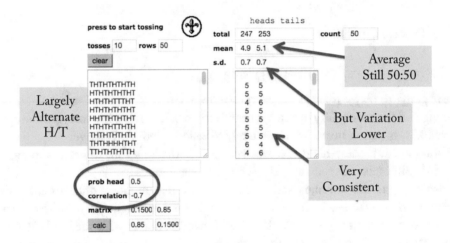

Figure 3.7: Negative correlation.

CHAPTER 4

Characterising the random through probability distributions

We now turn to distributions, another key word of statistics. You will probably at least have heard of the Normal distribution, the bell-shaped curve of many kinds of data, from heights of people to exam results (albeit the latter are occasionally forced!). All a 'distribution' means is the *different probabilities of different outcomes*.

4.1 TYPES OF PROBABILITY DISTRIBUTION

We will look at some of the different properties of data and distributions. We discuss the different kinds of continuous and discrete data and the way they may be bounded within some finite range, or be unbounded. In particular, we'll see how some kinds of data, such as income distributions, may have a very long tail, a small number of very large values. Some of this is a brief reprise if you have previously done some sort of statistics course.

4.1.1 CONTINUOUS OR DISCRETE?

One of the first things to consider before you start any statistical analysis is the kind of data you are dealing with.

A key difference is between continuous and discrete data. Think about an experiment where you have measured time taken to complete a particular sub-task and also the number of errors during the session. The first of these, completion time, is continuous. It might be 12 sec or 13 sec, but could also be 12.73 sec or anything in between. However, while a single user may have 12 or 13 errors, they cannot have 12.5 errors. Errors are discrete data.

Discrete values also come in a number of flavours.

The number of errors is arithmetical: the values can be meaningfully added or averaged. Although a single user cannot get 12.5 errors, it makes sense to average them, so you could find that the average error rate is 12.73 errors per user. Although one often jokes about the mythical family with 2.2 children, it is meaningful. If you have 100 families you expect, on average, 220 children. In survey data this is also sometimes called interval data.

In contrast, nominal or categorical data has discrete values that cannot easily be compared, added, or averaged. For example, if when presented with a menu half your users choose 'File' and half choose 'Font,' it does not make sense to say that they have on average selected 'Flml'!

In between are ordinal data, where there is an order, but otherwise no specific meaning to the values; for example the degrees of agreement or satisfaction in a Likert scale. A little confusingly these are often coded as numbers, so that 1 might be the left-most point and 5 the right-most point in a simple five-point Likert scale. While 5 may represent 'better than 4' and 3 'better than 2,' it is not necessarily the case that 4 is twice as good as 2. The points are ordered, but do not represent any precise values. Strictly you cannot simply add up and average ordinal values ... however, in practice and if you have enough data, you can sometimes 'get away' with it, especially if you just want an indicative idea or quick overview of data[1] ... but don't tell any purists I said so :-).

A special case of discrete data is binary data such as yes/no answers, or present/not present. Indeed one way to deal with ordinal data while avoiding frowned-upon averaging is to choose some critical value and turn the values into simple big/small. For example, you might say that 4 and 5 are generally 'satisfied,' so you convert 4 and 5 into 'Yes' and 1, 2, and 3 into 'No.' The downside of this is that it loses information, but it can be an easy way to present data.

4.1.2   FINITE OR UNBOUNDED

Another question about data is whether the values are finite or potentially unbounded. Let's look at some examples.

number of heads in 6 tosses – This is a discrete value and bounded. The valid responses can only be 0, 1, 2, 3, 4, 5, or 6. You cannot have 3.5 heads, nor can you have −3 heads, nor 7 heads.

number of heads until first tail – Still discrete, and still bounded below, but in this case unbounded above. Although unlikely, you could have to wait for 100 or 1000 heads before you get a tail. There is no absolute maximum, although once I got to 20 heads I might start to believe I was in the Matrix.

wait before next bus – This is now a continuous value: it could be 1 min, 20 min, or 12 min 17.36 sec. Like the previous example, it is bounded below (no negative wait times), but unbounded above: you could wait an hour, or even forever if they have cancelled the service.

difference between heights – If you had two buildings, Abbot Tower (let's say height A), and Burton Heights (height B), you could subtract A−B. If Abbot Tower is taller, the difference would be positive; if Burton Heights is taller, it would be negative. There are some physical limits on building height (if it were too tall the top part might be essentially in

---

[1]The reason this works is the Central Limit Theorem, which essentially says that averages of most things behave like a Normal distribution. We'll return to this in Section 4.2.2.

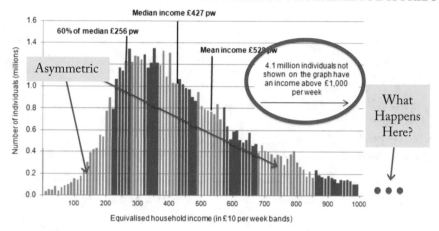

Figure 4.1: UK income distribution (source: [58]).

orbit and float away). However, for most purposes the difference is effectively unbounded, either building could be arbitrarily bigger than the other.

4.1.3   UK INCOME DISTRIBUTION – A LONG TAIL

Now for our first distribution (Fig. 4.1). The histogram is taken from UK Office for National Statistics data on weekly income during 2012. This is continuous data, but to plot it the ONS has put people into £10 'bins': 0–£9.99 in the first bin, £10–£19.99 in the next bin, etc.; the histogram height is the number of people who earn in that range.

Note that this is an empirical distribution, showing the actual number of people in each category, rather than a theoretical distribution based on mathematical calculations of probabilities.

You can easily see that mid-range weekly wages are around £300–£400, but with a lot of spread. Each bar in this mid-range represents a million people or so. Remembering my quick and dirty rule for count data (Section 2.2), the variability of each column is probably only +/- 2000, that is 0.2% of the column height. The columns that stick out of the curve are probably a real effect, not just random noise (yes, really an omen; at this scale things should be more uniform and smooth). I don't know the explanation, but I wonder if it is a small tendency for jobs to have weekly, monthly, or annual salaries that are round numbers.

You can also see that this is an asymmetric distribution: it rises quite rapidly from zero, but then tails off a lot more slowly. In fact, the rate of tailing off is so slow that the ONS have decided to cut it off at £1000 per week, even though it says that 4.1 million people earn more than this. In plotting the data they have chosen a cut off that avoids making the lower part too squashed. But how far out does the 'tail' go?

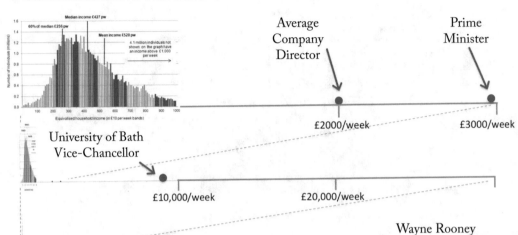

Figure 4.2: Long tail of large incomes.

I do not have the full data, but I assume the tail, the long spread of low frequency values, decays reasonably smoothly at first. However, I have found a few examples to populate a zoomed out view (Fig. 4.2). The examples are from 2017 rather than 2012, but due to the recession incomes did not vary greatly over that timescale.

At the top of Fig. 4.2 is the range expanded by 3 to go up to £3000 a week. On this I've put the average UK company director's salary of £2000 a week (£100K per annum) and the Prime Minister at about £3000 a week (£150K pa). UK professorial salaries fall roughly in the middle of this range.

The middle part of Fig. 4.2 zooms out by a factor of ten. The range is now up to £30,000 a week. About 1/3 of the way along is the then vice-chancellor of the University of Bath (effectively the CEO), who in 2017 was the highest paid university vice-chancellor in the UK at £450K pa, around three times more than the Prime Minister.

However, we can't stop here. If we zoom out by another factor of ten (bottom of Fig. 4.2) we can now see Wayne Rooney, who in 2017 was one of the highest paid footballers in the UK at £260,000 a week. Of course this is before we even get to the tech and property company super-rich who can earn (or at least amass) millions per week.

At this scale, look carefully at the far left. Can you just see a very thin spike of the mass of ordinary wage earners? This is why the ONS did not draw their histogram at this scale. This is a long-tail distribution, one where there are very high values but with very low frequency.

4.1.4   ONE TAIL OR TWO?

There is another use of the term 'tail' in statistics—you may have seen mention of one- or two-tailed tests. This refers to the same thing, the 'tail' of values at either end of a distribution, but in a slightly different way.

For a moment, forget the distribution of the values and think about the question you want to ask. Crucially, do you care about direction?

Imagine you are about to introduce a new system that has some additional functionality. However, you are worried that its additional complexity will make it more error prone. Before you deploy it you want to check this. Here your question is: "Is the error rate higher?" If it is actually lower that is nice, but you don't really care so long as it hasn't made things worse. This is a one-tailed test; you only care about one direction.

In contrast, imagine you are trying to decide between two systems, A and B. Before you make your decision you want to know whether the choice will affect performance, so you do a user test and measure completion times. This time your question is: "Are the completion times different?" This is a two-tailed test; you care in both directions: if A is better than B *and* if B is better than A.

4.2   NORMAL OR NOT?

Some phenomena, such as tossing coins, have well-understood distributions—in the case of coin tossing, the Binomial distribution. This means one can work out precisely how likely every outcome is. At other times we need to use an approximate distribution that is close enough.

The Normal distribution (the bell-shaped curve), also known as a Gaussian distribution, is a special case. Some phenomena such as heights seem to naturally follow this distribution, whilst others, including the (Binomial) coin-toss scores, end up looking approximately Normal for sufficiently many tosses.

However, there are special reasons why this works and there are some phenomena, including income distributions and social network data, which are definitely *not* Normal!

4.2.1   APPROXIMATIONS

Often in statistics, and also in engineering and forms of applied mathematics, one thing can be approximated by another. For example, when working out the deflection of a beam under small loads, it is common to assume it takes on a circular arc shape, when in fact the actual shape is somewhat more complex.

Figure 4.3 shows a histogram. It is a theoretical distribution, the Binomial distribution for $n = 6$. This is what you'd expect for the number of heads if you tossed a fair coin six times. The histogram has been worked out from the maths: for $n = 1$ (one toss) it would have been 50:50 for 0 and 1. If it was $n = 2$ (two tosses), the histogram would have been ¼, ½, ¼ for 0,1,2. For $n = 6$, the probabilities are 1/64, 6/64, 15/64, 20/64, 15/64, 6/64, 1/64 for 0–6. However, if you

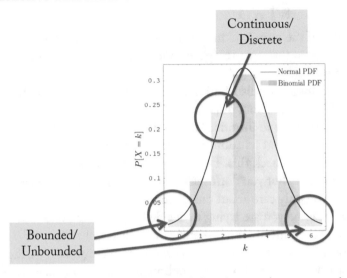

Figure 4.3: Normal approximation of the Binomial distribution (coin tossing) (source: `https://commons.wikimedia.org/wiki/File:Binomial_Distribution.svg`).

tossed six coins, then did it again and again and again, thousands of times, and kept tally of the number you got, you would end up getting closer and closer to this theoretical distribution.

It is discrete and bounded, but overlaid on it is a line representing the Normal distribution with mean and standard deviation chosen to match the Binomial. The Normal distribution is a continuous distribution and unbounded (the tails go on for ever), but is actually not a bad fit, and for some purposes may be good enough.

In fact, if you look at the same curves against a Binomial for 20, 50, or 100 tosses, the match gets better and better. As many statistical tests (such as Student's t-test, linear regression, and ANOVA) are based around the Normal, this is good news; it means you can often use these tests even with something such as coin tossing data.

4.2.2   THE CENTRAL LIMIT THEOREM – (NEARLY) EVERYTHING IS NORMAL

Although doing statistics on coin tosses is not particularly helpful, except in exercises, coin tosses are not the only thing to come out approximately Normal; many measurements, from people's heights to exam results, seem to follow the Normal curve. Why is that?

A mathematical result, the central limit theorem, explains why this happens. It says that if you take lots of items then the average (arithmetic mean) or sum of lots of very small things behaves more and more like a Normal distribution as the number of small items gets larger.

However, this only happens if the following conditions hold.

1. You **average them** or add them up (or do something close to linear).

2. They are **around the same size** (so no single value dominates).

3. They are **nearly independent** (as discussed in Section 3.2).

4. They have **finite variance** (discussed below).

As an example, our height is based on many genes and many environmental factors. Occasionally, for some individuals, there may be a single rare gene condition, traumatic event, or illness that stunts growth or causes gigantism. However, for the majority of the population it is the cumulative effect (near sum) of all those small effects that leads to our ultimate height, and that is why height is Normally distributed.

Indeed, this pattern of large numbers of small things is so common that we find Normal distributions everywhere.

4.2.3 NON-NORMAL – WHAT CAN GO WRONG?

So, given this set of conditions is so common, does *everything* become Normal so long as you average enough of them?

Well, if you look through the conditions, various things can go wrong.

Condition (2), not having a single overwhelming value, is fairly obvious, and you can see when it is likely to fail.

The independence condition (3) is actually not as demanding as first appears. In the virtual coin demonstrator, setting a high correlation between coin tosses meant you got long runs of heads or tails, but eventually you get a swap and then a run of the other side. Although 'enough of them' ends up being even more things to average, you still get Normal distributions *eventually*. Here the non-independence is local and fades; all that matters is that there are no long-distance effects so that one value does not affect so many of the others as to dominate. More problematic is if there is a single factor that links all the data, for example a sampling bias as discussed in Section 3.2.

The linearity condition (1) is more interesting. There are various things that can cause nonlinearity. One is some sort of threshold effect; for example, if plants are growing near an electric fence, those that reach a certain height may simply be electrocuted, leading to a chopped-off Normal distribution!

Feedback effects also cause nonlinearity, because some initial change can make huge differences, the well-known butterfly effect. Snowflake growth is a good example of positive feedback. Ice forms more easily on sharp tips, so any small growth grows further and ends up being a long spike. In contrast, child's-picture-book bumpy clouds suggest a negative feedback process that smooths out any protuberances.

In education, in some subjects, particularly mathematical or more theoretical computer science, the exam results end up not as a Normal-like bell curve, but with two humps (bimodal) as if there were two groups of students. There are various reasons for this, not least of which is the tendency for many subjects like this to have questions with an 'easy bit' and then a 'sting in the tail!' However, this may also represent a true split in the student population. In the humanities, if you have trouble with one week's lectures, you can still understand the next week. With mathematical topics, often once you lose track everything else seems incomprehensible. This is a positive feedback process: one small failure leads to a bigger failure, and so on.

However, condition (4), the finite variance, is the most odd. Variance is a measure of the spread of a distribution. You find the variance by first finding the arithmetic mean of your data, then working out the differences from this (called the residuals), square those differences and then find the average of those squares.

For any real set of data this is bound to be a finite number, so what does it mean to not have a finite variance?

Normally, if you take larger and larger samples, this variance figure settles down and gets closer and closer to a single value. Try this with the virtual coin tossing application. Increase the number of rows and watch the figure for the standard deviation (square root of variance) gradually settle down to a stable (and finite) value.

However, there are some phenomena where if you did this, took larger and larger samples, the standard deviation would not settle down to a final value, but would instead typically get larger and larger as the sample size grows (although, as this is random, sometimes larger samples might have a small spread). The variance and standard deviation are finite for any single finite sample, but they grow unboundedly large as samples get larger.

Whether this happens or not is all about the tail. It is only possible at all with an unbounded tail, where there are occasional very large values, but on its own this is not sufficient.

Take the example of the number of heads you toss before you get a tail (called a Negative Binomial). This is unbounded, you could get any number of heads, but the likelihood of getting lots of heads falls off very rapidly (one in a million for 20 heads), which leads to a finite mean of 1 and a finite variance of exactly 2.

Similarly, the Normal distribution itself has potentially unbounded values, arbitrarily large in positive and/or negative directions, but they are very unlikely, resulting in a finite variance.

Indeed, in my early career distributions without finite variance seemed relatively rare, a curiosity. One of the few common examples was income distributions in economics. For income, the few super-rich are often not enough to skew the arithmetic average income. In the earlier example, even Wayne Rooney's wages averaged over the entire UK working population are less than a penny each. However, those few very well-paid individuals are enough to affect variance. Of course, for any set of people at any time, the variance is still finite, but the shape of it means that, in practice, if you take lots of samples of first, say, 100, then 1000, then larger and larger, the variance will keep on going up. For wealth (rather than income) this is also true for the average!

I said 'in my early career,' as this (in the 1980s) was before the realisation of how common power law distributions were in human and natural phenomena.

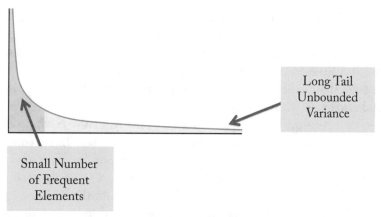

Figure 4.4: Power law distribution (source: https://en.wikipedia.org/wiki/Power_law).

4.2.4   POWER LAW DISTRIBUTIONS

You may have heard of the phrase 'power law' or maybe 'scale free' distributions, particularly related to web phenomena. Do note that the use of the term 'power' here is different from statistical 'power,' and for that matter the Power Rangers.

Some years ago it became clear that a number of physical phenomena, for example earthquakes, have behaviours that are very different from the Normal distribution or other distributions that were commonly dealt with in statistics at that time [72].

An example that you can observe for yourself is the simple egg timer. Watch the sand grains as they dribble through the hole and land in a pile below. The pile initially grows, the small pile gets steeper and steeper, and then there is a little landslide and the top of the pile levels a little, then grows again, another little landslide. If you kept track of the landslides, some would be small, just levelling off the very tip of the pile, some larger, and sometimes the whole side of the pile cleaves away.

There is a largest size for the biggest landslide due to the small size of the egg timer, but if you imagine the same slow stream of sand falling onto a larger pile, you can imagine even larger landslides.

If you keep track of the size of landslides, there are fewer large landslides than smaller ones, but the fall off is not nearly as dramatic as, say, the likelihood of getting lots and lots of heads in a row when tossing a coin. Like the income distribution, the distribution is 'tail heavy;' there are enough low frequency but very high value events to affect the variance.

For sand piles and for earthquakes, this is due to positive feedback effects. Think of dropping a single grain of sand on the pile. Sometimes it just lands and stays. While the sand pile is quite shallow this happens most of the time and the pile just gets higher … and steeper. However, when the pile is of a critical size and steepness, when the slope is only just stable, sometimes the single grain knocks another out of place. These may both roll a little and then stop, or they may knock yet more grains. The little landslide has enough speed to create a larger one.

Earthquakes are just the same. Tension builds up in the rocks, and at some stage a part of the fault that is a little loose, or under slightly more tension, gives way—a minor quake. However, sometimes that small amount of release means the bit of fault next to it is pushed over its own limit and also gives: the quake gets bigger, and so on.

User interface testing and user experience testing rarely involve earthquakes, nor for that matter sand piles. However, network phenomena such as web page links, paper citations and social media connections follow a very similar pattern. The reason for this is again positive feed-back effects: if a web page has lots of links to it, or a paper is heavily cited, others are more likely to find it and so link to it or cite it further. Small differences in the engagement or quality of the source, or simply some random initial spark of interest, lead to large differences in the final link/citation count. Similarly, if you have lots of Twitter followers, more people see your tweets and choose to follow you.

Crucially, this means that if you take the number of citations of a paper, or the number of social media connections of a person, these do *not* behave like a Normal distribution even when averaged. So, if you use statistical tests and tools that assume Normal data, such as t-tests, ANOVA, or linear regression, your analysis will be utterly meaningless and quite likely misleading.

As this kind of data becomes more common it is increasingly important to understand the limits of the 'Normal' distribution and when you need to seek other forms of statistics.

This does not mean you cannot use this sort of data, but you must use special tests for it, or process the data to make it amenable to standard tests. For example, you can take citation or social network connection data and code each as 'low' (bottom quartile of citations/connections), medium (middle 50%), or high (top quartile of citations/connections). If you turn these into a 0, 1, 2 scale, these have relative probability 0.25, 0.5, 0.25—just like the number of heads when tossing two coins. This transformation of the data means that it is now suitable for use with standard tests so long as you have sufficient measurements—which is usually not a problem with this kind of data!

4.2.5   PARAMETRIC AND NONPARAMETRIC

In some cases the phenomenon we are interested in falls into one of the well-known theoretical distributions: counts of coin tosses follow a Binomial distribution, human heights are Normal, and wait times between incoming phone calls at a call centre follow the Poisson distribution.

In these cases there are often well-established techniques relying on the mathematics of the relevant distribution. For example, simple linear regression techniques (when you look for a best-fit line through scattered data points) assume a Normal distribution of measurement errors. In other cases, we either do not know the distribution or there are no established techniques for it.

This leads to two broad classes of statistical techniques.

Parametric – This is where we have a known theoretical distribution, but just need to estimate a few unknown parameters. For example, we may believe that people's heights are Normally distributed, but not know their average height (μ) and its standard deviation (σ), or we know that successive coin tosses are independent two-outcome events (and therefore follow the Binomial distribution), but do not know whether the coin is biased (p, the probability of a head, is unknown).

Nonparametric – This is where we have no such model (or it is too complex), and instead we rely on universal properties such as the ordering of values. For example, suppose we run a study with 20 users: 10 using system A and 10 system B. When we analyse the results, we find that all of the completion times for system A are lower than those for system B. We can work out how likely this is[2] without knowing anything about the shape of the exact distribution of times (which are typically not Normal).

Statisticians prefer to use parametric statistics where possible. This is because you are using more of the available information (you know the distribution) and hence the statistics have greater power, that is you are less likely to miss a real effect; there are fewer false negatives.

In the case of the power law, we saw that transforming data can produce a more tractable distribution. The transformation to quartiles is a generic technique, which can be applied to any form of data, not just power laws. It is effectively a form of nonparametric statistic. However, some transformations can allow the use of more powerful parametric techniques.

One example where data transformations can be very effective is for task completion times. These are clearly not Normally distributed as they are bounded below (no negative times). If the average time is large compared with the standard deviation, it can be that the data is near enough to Normal for standard tests to be used. However, if the spread is large compared with the average time, the graph is typically very asymmetric and Normal tests cannot be used. However, in these cases, if you take the logarithm of the raw times (which sends 0 off to minus infinity), the resulting transformed data is often Normal and can then be analysed using off-the-shelf statistics. For obvious reasons, this is called a Log-Normal distribution and is common where there is some form of multiplicative effect.

---

[2]Less than 1 in 100,000, extremely significant.

PART II

Doing It – If not p then What

CHAPTER 5

Probing the unknown

You use statistics when there is something in the world you don't know, and you want to get a level of quantified understanding of it based on some form of the measurement or sample.

The following chapters will discuss three major kinds of statistical analysis methods.

Hypothesis testing (the dreaded p!) – robust but confusing.

Confidence intervals – powerful but underused.

Bayesian statistics – mathematically clean but fragile.

The first two use essentially the same theoretical approach; the difference is more about the way you present results. Bayesian statistics takes a fundamentally different approach, with its own strengths and weaknesses.

One key mathematical element shared by all these techniques is the idea of conditional probability and likelihood: the probability of a specific measurement occurring, assuming you know everything pertinent about the real world. Of course the whole point is that you don't know what is true of the real world, but you do know about the measurement, so you need to do back-to-front reasoning to go back from measurement to the world!

5.1 RECALL ... THE JOB OF STATISTICS

First of all let's recall the 'job of statistics' (Fig. 5.1), which is an attempt to understand the fundamental properties of the real world based on measurements and samples. For example, you may have taken a dozen people (the sample) and asked them to perform the same task on a new and an old version of some software. You have recorded response times, satisfaction, error rate, etc., (the measurement) and you want to know whether your new software will outperform the original software for the whole user group (the real world).

5.2 CONDITIONAL PROBABILITY

We are dealing with data where the measurements include some level of randomness (of the various kinds described in Section 1.3.3) and so we need to deal with probabilities, but in particular what is known as conditional probability.

Imagine the main street of a local city. What is the probability that it is busy? Now imagine that you are standing in the same street but it is 4 AM on a Sunday morning: what is the

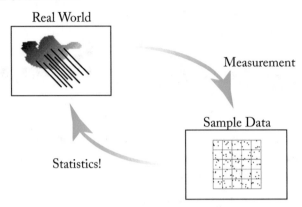

Figure 5.1: The job of statistics (from Chapter 1).

probability that it is busy given the time of day? Although the overall probability of it being busy (at a random time of day) is high, the probability that it is busy *given* it is 4 AM on a Sunday is lower.

Similarly, think of throwing a single die. What is the probability it is a six? 1 in 6. However, if I peek and tell you it is at least a four, what is the probability now that it is a six? The probability it is a six *given* it is four or greater is 1 in 3.

When we have more information, then we change our assessment of the probability of events accordingly. This calculation of probability *given* some information is what mathematicians call conditional probability.

5.3   LIKELIHOOD

Returning again to the job of statistics, we are interested in the relationship between measurements of the real world and what is true of the real world. Although we may not know what is true of the world (for example, what the actual error rate of our new software is going to be), we can often work out the conditional probability of measurements given the (unknown) state of the world.

For example, if the probability of a single user making a particular error is 1 in 10, then the probability that exactly 2 make the error out of a sample of 5 is 7.29% (calculated from the Binomial distribution).

This conditional probability of a measurement given an hypothetical state of the world (or typically some specific parameters of the world) is what statisticians call likelihood.

As another example, the probability that six tosses of a coin will come out heads given the coin is fair is 1/64, or in other words the likelihood that it is fair is 1/64. If instead the coin were biased 2/3 heads 1/3 tails, the probability of six heads given this (that is the likelihood of the coin having this bias) is 64/729 ~ 1/11.

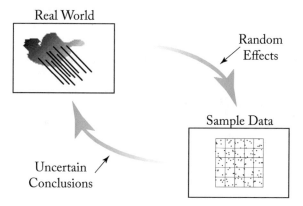

Figure 5.2: Statistical reasoning: seeing past random effects to reach uncertain conclusions.

Note this likelihood is *not* the probability that the coin is fair or biased; we may have good reason to believe that most coins are fair. However, it does constitute *evidence*. The core difference between different kinds of statistics is the way this evidence is used.

Effectively statistics tries to turn this process round, to take the likelihood, the probability of the measurement given the unknown state of the world, and reverse it, using the fact that the measurement has occurred to tell us something about the world.

5.4   STATISTICAL REASONING

Going back again to the job of statistics, the measurements we have of the world are prone to all sorts of random effects (Fig. 5.2). The likelihood models the impact of these random effects as probabilities. The different types of statistics then use this to produce conclusions about the real world.

However, crucially these are always *uncertain conclusions*. Although we can improve our ability to see through the fog of randomness, there is always the possibility that by sheer chance things appear to suggest one conclusion even though it is not true.

Note also that this form of reasoning is counterfactual, that is you often have to work with states of the world about which you are agnostic or even believe to be false. For example, suppose you have a new redesigned interface that you have been working on for the last six months and are now evaluating in a user trial. Even though you believe it is better, you need to temporarily assume that the new interface is actually worse than the old one, in order to calculate the likelihood of the results of the user trial given that assumption.

In summary:

likelihood is the conditional probability of obtaining particular measurements given potential states of the world

statistics turns this on its head: given actual measurements it creates uncertain knowledge of the unknown world

5.5   TYPES OF STATISTICS

We will now focus on the three major types of statistics.

Hypothesis testing – This is what you are most likely to have seen—the dreaded p-value! It was originally introduced as a form of "quick hack," but has come to be the most widely used tool. Although it can be misused, deliberately or accidentally, in many ways, it is time-tested, robust and quite conservative. The downside is that understanding what it really says (*not* $p < 5\%$ means true!) can be slightly complex.

Confidence intervals – This approach uses the same underlying mathematical methods as hypothesis testing, but instead of talking about whether there is evidence for or against a single value, or proposition, confidence intervals give a range of values. This is really powerful in giving a sense of the level of uncertainty around an estimate or prediction; unfortunately, confidence levels are woefully underused.

Bayesian statistics – This method uses the same underlying likelihood (although it is not called that!) but combines it with numerical estimates of the probability of the world. It is mathematically very clean, but can be fragile. One needs to be particularly careful to avoid confirmation bias, and also when dealing with multiple sources of non-independent evidence. In addition, because the results are expressed as probabilities, Bayesian statistics may give an impression of objectivity, but in most cases it is really about modifying one's assessment of belief.

We will look at each of these in more detail in the following chapters.

To some extent these techniques have been pretty much the same for the past 50 years; however, computation has gradually made differences. Crucially, early statistics needed to be relatively easy to calculate by hand, whereas computer-based statistical analyses remove this constraint. One example of this is the use of fixed p-values (5%, 1%, etc.). Previously statistical tables had to be laboriously compiled; now exact values (e.g., $p = 0.2736$) are often provided by statistical programs. In addition, the growing power of computers has allowed more complex models based on theoretical distributions, and also simulation methods that use models where there is no 'nice' mathematical solution.

CHAPTER 6

Traditional statistics

In this chapter we'll look at the first two kinds of statistics: hypothesis testing and confidence intervals. These use the same underlying mathematics and share a common philosophical stance. They are the techniques you will encounter most often in the scientific literature.

6.1 HYPOTHESIS TESTING

Hypothesis testing is still the most common use of statistics. You will have seen it used in papers and reports and may well have used it yourself. It uses various methods and measures to come up with the common $p < 5\%$ or $p < 1\%$ result.

We'll look at what this 5% (or 1%) actually means and, just as important, what it does *not* mean. Perhaps even more critical is to understand what you can and cannot conclude from a non-significant result, and in particular to remember that such a result means 'not proven' *not* 'no effect!'

The language of hypothesis testing can be a little opaque. A core term, which you have probably seen, is the idea of the null hypothesis, also written H_0, which is usually what you want to disprove. For example, H_0 might be that your new software design has made no difference to error rates. In contrast, the alternative hypothesis, written H_1, is what you typically would like to be true.

The argument form is similar to proof by contradiction in logic or mathematics. In this you assert what you believe to be false as if it were true, reason from that to something that is clearly contradictory, and then use the contradiction to argue that what you first asserted must indeed be false.

In statistical reasoning of course you don't *know* that something is false, just that it is unlikely. The hypothesis testing reasoning goes like this:

if the null hypothesis H_0 were true

then the observations (measurements) are very unlikely

therefore the null hypothesis H_0 is (likely to be) false and hence the alternative H_1 is (likely to be) true

For example, imagine our null hypothesis is that a coin is fair. You toss it 100 times and it ends up a head every time. The probability of this given a fair coin (likelihood) is $1/2^{100}$ that is around 1 in a nonillion (1 with 30 zeros). This seems so unlikely, you begin to wonder about that coin!

6.1.1   THE SIGNIFICANCE LEVEL – 5 PERCENT AND ALL THAT

Of course, most experiments are not as clear cut as that. You may have heard of the term significance level. This is the threshold at which you decide to reject the null hypothesis. In the example above, the significance level was 1 in a nonillion, but that is quite extreme.

The smallest significance level that is normally regarded as reasonable evidence is 5%. This means that if the likelihood of the null hypothesis (probability of the observation given H_0) is less than 5% (1 in 20), you 'reject' it and assume the alternative must be true. By 'assume' I mean that you decide that the given level is *sufficient evidence* for you to continue, but, as we shall see, this *does not mean* that there a high probability that the alternative is true or false, merely that the null hypothesis is unlikely to have given rise to the observed results.

Returning to our software design example, let's say that our null hypothesis was that your new design is no different to the old one. When you tested with six users all the users preferred the new design. The reasoning using a 5% significance level as a threshold would go:

if the null hypothesis H_0 is true (no difference)

then the probability of the observed effect (6 preferences) happening by chance is 1/64 which is less than 5%

therefore reject H_0 as unlikely to be true and conclude that the alternative H_1 is likely to be true

Yay! your new design is better :)

Note that this significance level of 5% is fairly arbitrary. What significance level is acceptable depends on a lot of factors. In usability, we will typically be using the results of the experiment alongside other evidence, often knowing that we need to make adaptations to generalise beyond the conditions. In physics, if they conclude something is true, it is taken to be incontrovertibly true, so they look for a figure more like 1 in several million.

Note too that if you take 5% as your acceptable significance level, then even if your new design were no better there would still be a 1 in 20 chance you would conclude it was better—statisticians call this a type I error; more comprehensibly, it is a false positive result.

6.1.2   BUT WHAT DOES IT MEAN?

A 5% significance does *not* say that the probability of the null hypothesis is less than 1 in 20. Think about the coin you are tossing: it is either fair or not fair; or think of the experiment comparing your new design with the old one: your design either is or is not better in terms of error rate for typical users.

Similarly, it does not say the probability of the alternative hypothesis (your new system is better) is > 0.95. Again that either is true or is not.

Nor does it say that the difference is *important*. Imagine you have lots and lots of participants in an experiment, so many that you are able to distinguish quite small differences. The experiment shows, with a high degree of statistical significance (maybe 0.1%), that users perform faster with your new system than the old one. The difference turns out to be 0.03 sec over an average time of 73 sec. The difference is real and reliable, but do you care?

So much for what the 5% or 1% significance level does not say about the world; what does it allow you to conclude?

All that a 5% significance level says is that if the null hypothesis H_0 were true, then the probability of seeing the observed outcome by chance is 1 in 20. Similarly for a 1% level the probability of seeing the observed outcome by chance is 1 in 100, etc.

6.1.3   NON-SIGNIFICANT RESULTS

Perhaps the easiest mistake to make with hypothesis testing occurs not when the result is significant, but when it isn't.

Say you have run your experiment comparing your old software system with the new design and there is no statistically significant difference between the two. Does that mean there is no difference? This is a possible explanation, but it may also simply mean that your experiment was not good enough to detect the difference.

Although you do reason that a significant result means the H_0 is false and H_1 (the alternative) is likely to be true, you cannot do the opposite. You can *never* (simply) reason: a non-significant result means H_0 is true / H_1 is false.

For example, imagine we have tossed a coin four times and all came up heads. If the coin is fair the probability of this happening is 1 in 16, which is not < 5%, so even with the least strict significance level, the result is not statistically significant. However, this was the most extreme result that was possible given the experiment; four coin tosses could never give you enough information to reject the null hypothesis of a fair coin!

Scottish law courts can return three verdicts: guilty, not guilty or not proven. Guilty means the judge or jury feels there is enough evidence to conclude reasonably that the accused did the crime (but of course they could still be wrong), and not guilty means they are reasonably certain the accused did not commit the crime. The 'not proven' verdict means that the judge or jury simply does not feel they have sufficient evidence to say one way or the other. This is often the verdict when it is a matter of the victim's word versus that of the accused, as frequently happens in rape cases.

Scotland is unusual in having the three classes of verdict and there is some debate about whether to remove the 'not proven' verdict, as in practice both 'not proven' and 'not guilty' mean the accused is acquitted. However, it highlights that in other jurisdictions 'not guilty' includes both: it does not mean the court is necessarily convinced that the accused is innocent, merely that the prosecution has not provided sufficient evidence to prove they are guilty. In general, a court would prefer the guilty to walk free than the innocent to be incarcerated, so the barrier to declaring 'guilty' is high ('beyond all reasonable doubt' … not $p < 5\%$!); amongst the 'not guilty' will be many who committed a crime as well as many who did not.

In statistics 'not significant' is just the same: 'not proven.'

6.1.4   IN SUMMARY—SIGNIFICANCE

In summary, all a test of statistical significance means is that if the null hypothesis (often no difference) is true, then the probability of seeing the measured results is low (e.g., < 5%, or < 1%). This is then used as evidence against the null hypothesis. It is good to remind ourselves of this occasionally, but for most purposes an informal understanding is that statistical significance is evidence for the alternative hypothesis (often what you are trying to show), but may be wrong—and the smaller the % or probability, the more reliable the result. However, all that non-significance tells you is that you have neither proved nor disproved your hypothesis.

So if you obtain a 5% significant result

it does **not** say
+ the probability of H_0 is < 1 in 20
+ the probability of H_1 is > 0.95
+ the effect is large or important

all it says is
V if H_0 were true …
… the observations are unlikely (prob. < 1 in 20)

If your results are non-significant:

you can **never** reason
+ non-significant result $\Rightarrow$ H_1 is false

all you can say is
V H_1 is not statistically proven

A QUICK EXPERIMENT

Here is a small exercise to get a feeling for that $p < 5\%$ figure ... are your coins really fair?

Choose a coin, any coin. If a coin is fair then the probability of six heads in a row is 1/64 as is the probability of six tails, and the probability of six of either is 2/64, approximately 3%. So we can do an experiment.

H_0 – the null hypothesis is that the coin is fair.

H_1 – the alternative hypothesis is that the coin is not fair.

The likelihood of HHHHHH or TTTTTT given H_0 is less than 5%, so if you get six heads or six tails, you can reject the null hypothesis and conclude that the coin is not fair. Try it, and if it doesn't work try again. How long before you end up with a 'statistically significant' test?

This might seem a little artificial, but imagine rather than coin tossing you have six user's preferences for software A or B. Having done this, how do you feel about whether 5% is a suitable level to regard as evidence? We will return to this issue when we discuss cherry picking and multiple tests in Chapter 8.

6.2 CONFIDENCE INTERVALS

Significance testing helps us to tell the difference between a real effect and random-chance patterns, but it is less helpful in giving us a clear idea of the potential size of an effect, and most importantly putting bounds on how similar things are. Confidence intervals help with both of these, giving some idea of where real values or real differences lie.

So you ran your experiment, you compared user response times in a suite of standard tasks, worked out the statistics and it came out not significant—unproven.

As we've seen, this does not allow us to conclude there is no difference, it just may be that the difference was too small to see given the level of experimental error. Of course this error may be large, for example if we have few participants and there is a lot of individual difference; so even a large difference may be missed.

How can we tell the difference between not proven and no difference?

In fact, it is usually impossible to say definitively 'no difference' as there may always be vanishingly small differences that we cannot detect. However, we can put *bounds* on inequality.

6.2.1   THE INTERVAL

A confidence interval does precisely this. It uses the same information and mathematics as are used to generate the p-values in a significance test, but then uses them to create a lower and upper bound on the true value.

For example, we may have measured the response times in the old and new software systems and found an average difference of 0.3 sec, but this did not turn out to be a statistically significant difference.

On its own this puts us in the 'not proven' territory: simply unknown. However, we can also ask our statistics application to calculate a 95% confidence interval. Let's say this turns out to be [-0.7,1.3] (often, but not always, these are symmetric around the average value). Informally, this gives us an idea of the level of uncertainty about the average. Note that this suggests it may be as low as -0.7, that is our new system may be up to 0.7 sec slower than the old system, but it may also be up to 1.3 sec faster. However, like everything in statistics, this is uncertain knowledge.

Note that this is the special case of a confidence interval on the difference of two things, so that the zero value means 'no difference.' This is a common case when performing comparative tests. In other cases the confidence interval is on an absolute measurement, for example estimating the time taken to navigate a website.

What the 95% confidence interval actually says is that if the true value were outside the range, then the probability of seeing the observed outcome is less than 5%. In other words, if our null hypothesis had been "the difference is 2 sec," or "the difference is 1.4 sec," or "the difference is 0.8 sec the other way," in all of these cases the probability of the outcome would be less than 5%.

By a similar reasoning to that of the significance testing, this is then taken as evidence that the true value really is in the range.

For the case of a confidence interval of a difference, zero is within the 95% confidence range precisely when the result is deemed non-significant at the 5% level. Similarly, if zero is outside the confidence interval, then the result is significant at 5%. The additional information the confidence interval gives is the potential size of the difference.

Of course, 5% is a low degree of evidence; maybe you would prefer a 99% confidence interval, which then means that if the true value were outside the interval, the probability of seeing the observed outcome is less than 1 in 100. This 99% confidence interval will be wider than the 95% one, perhaps [-1,1.6]; if you want to be more certain that the value is in a range, the range becomes wider.

Just like significance testing, the 95% confidence interval of [-0.7,1.3] does not say that there is a 95% probability that the real value is in the range: it either is or it is not. All it says is that if the real value were to lie outside the range, then the probability of the outcome is less than 5% (or 1% for a 99% confidence interval).

6.2.2   IMPORTANT AS WELL AS SIGNIFICANT?

Let's say we ran our experiment as described and it had a mean difference in response time of 0.3 sec, which was not significant, even at 5%. At this point, we still had no idea of whether this indicated no (important) difference or simply a poor experiment. Things were inconclusive.

However, we then worked out the 95% confidence interval to be [-0.7,1.3]. Now we can start to make some stronger statements.

The upper limit of the confidence interval is 1.3 sec; that is we have a reasonable level of confidence that the real difference is no bigger than this—does it matter, is this an *important difference*? The answer lies not in the numbers from the statistics, but in understanding your problem domain. Imagine this is a 1.3 sec difference on a two-hour task, and that deploying the new system would cost millions: it would probably not be worth it.

Equally, if there were other reasons for wanting to deploy the system, would it matter if it were 0.7 sec slower?

We had to ask precisely this question with a novel soft keyboard for mobile phones some years ago [39]. The keyboard could be overlaid on top of content, but leaving the content visible, so it had clear advantages in that respect over a standard soft keyboard that takes up the lower part of the screen. My colleague ran an experiment and found that the new keyboard was slower (by around 10 sec in a 100 sec task), and that this difference was statistically significant.

If our goal had been to improve the speed of entry this would have been a real problem for the design. In fact we had expected it to be a little slower, partly because it was novel and therefore unfamiliar. Furthermore, the design had other advantages, so though it was important that the novel keyboard was not massively slower, a small loss of speed was acceptable.

We calculated the 95% confidence interval for the slowdown at [2s,18s]. That is we could be fairly confident it was at least 2 sec slower, but also confident that it was no more than 18 sec slower in the 100-sec task.

Note that this is different from the previous examples. Here we have a significant difference, but we are using the confidence interval to give us an idea of how big that difference is. In this case, we have good evidence that the slow-down was no more than about 20%, which was acceptable.

6.2.3   DON'T FORGET …

Researchers are often more familiar with significance testing and know that they need to quote the number of participants, the test used, etc. You can see this in (nearly) every report you have read that uses statistics.

When you quote a confidence interval the same applies. If the data is two-outcome true/false data (like the coin toss), then the confidence interval may have been calculated using the Binomial distribution; if it is people's heights it might use the Normal distribution or Student's T distribution—this needs to be reported so that others can verify the calculations, or maybe reproduce your results.

Finally, do remember that, as with all statistics, the confidence interval is still *uncertain*. It offers good evidence that the real value is within the interval, but it could still be outside.

CHAPTER 7

Bayesian methods

Bayesian reasoning allows one to make strong statements about the probability of things based on evidence. This can be used for internal algorithms, for example to make adaptive or intelligent interfaces. It can also be used in a form of statistical reasoning, Bayesian statistics, which can be used as an alternative to traditional hypothesis testing or other statistical analyses.

However, to do this you need to be able to quantify in a robust and defensible manner what are the expected 'prior probabilities' of different hypotheses before an experiment. This holds the potential danger of confirmation bias, simply finding the results you thought of before you started, but when there are solid grounds for those estimates it is both precise and powerful.

Crucially, it is important to remember that Bayesian statistics is ultimately about quantified belief, not probability.

7.1 DETECTING THE MARTIAN INVASION

It is common knowledge that all Martians have antennae (just watch a sci-fi B-movie). However, humans rarely do; perhaps if there is some rare genetic condition or occasional fancy dress, so let's say the probability that a human has antennae is no more than 1 in a 1000 (Fig. 7.1).

You decide to conduct a small experiment. There are two hypotheses.

H_0 – there are no Martians in the High Street

H_1 – the Martians have landed

You go out into the High Street and the first person you meet has antennae. The probability of this occurring given the null hypothesis that there are no Martians in the High Street is 1 in 1000, so we can reject the null hypothesis at $p \leq 0.1\%$ ... which is a far stronger result than you are likely to see in most usability experiments.

Should you call the Men in Black?

For a more familiar example, let's go back to the coin tossing. You pull a coin out of your pocket, toss it 10 times and it is a head every time. The chances of this given it is a fair coin are just 1 in 1000; do you assume that the coin is fixed or that it is just a fluke? Instead imagine it is not a coin from your pocket, but a coin from a stallholder at a street market running a gambling game—the coin lands heads 10 times in a row; do you trust this coin more or less?

Now imagine it is a usability test and ten users were asked to compare an original system with a new version that you have spent many weeks perfecting. All ten users said they prefer the new system ... what do you think about that? Is it convincing evidence?

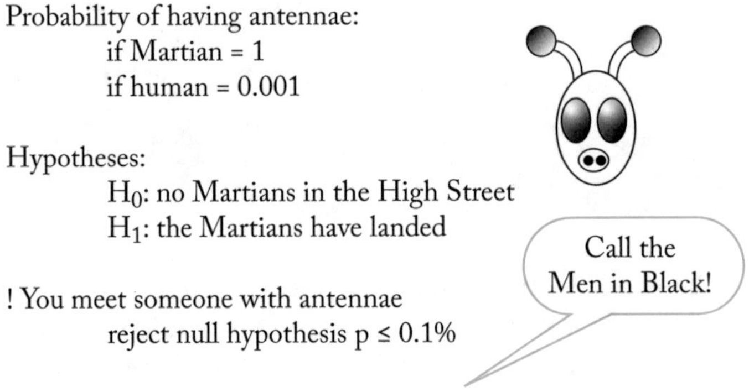

Probability of having antennae:
    if Martian = 1
    if human = 0.001

Hypotheses:
    H_0: no Martians in the High Street
    H_1: the Martians have landed

! You meet someone with antennae
    reject null hypothesis p ≤ 0.1%

Call the
Men in Black!

Figure 7.1: Traditional statistics—Is it a Martian?

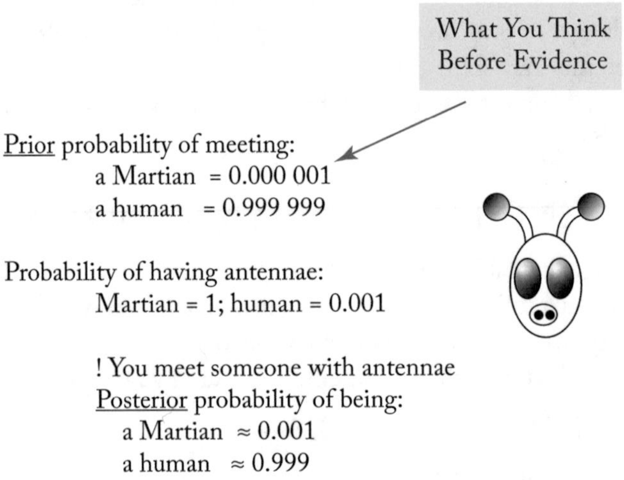

What You Think
Before Evidence

<u>Prior</u> probability of meeting:
    a Martian = 0.000 001
    a human   = 0.999 999

Probability of having antennae:
    Martian = 1; human = 0.001

! You meet someone with antennae
<u>Posterior</u> probability of being:
    a Martian ≈ 0.001
    a human   ≈ 0.999

Figure 7.2: The Bayesian approach to meeting a Martian.

7.2   QUANTIFYING PRIOR BELIEF

Clearly in day-to-day reasoning we take into account our prior beliefs and use that alongside the evidence from the observations we have made. Bayesian reasoning tries to quantify this. You turn that vague feeling that it is unlikely you will meet a Martian, or unlikely the coin is biased, into solid numbers—your belief is *encoded* as a probability.

Let's go back to the Martian example, but we'll take a Bayesian approach to the problem (Fig. 7.2). We know we are unlikely to meet a Martian, but how unlikely? We need to make an estimate of this prior probability, let's say it is a million to one.

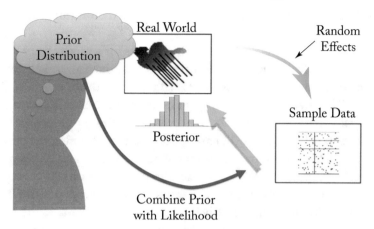

Figure 7.3: Bayesian inference.

prior probability of meeting a Martian = 0.000001

prior probability of meeting a human = 0.999999

Remember that all Martians have antennae so the probability that someone we meet has antennae given they are Martian is 1, and we said the probability of antennae given they are human was 0.001 (allowing for dressing up).

Now, just as in the previous scenario, you go out into the High Street and the first person you meet has antennae. You combine this information: the observed evidence, the prior probability and the conditional probabilities given the person is Martian or human (likelihood), to end up with a revised posterior probability of each:

posterior probability that the person is a Martian ~ 0.001

posterior probability that the person is a human ~ 0.999

We'll see the exact maths for a similar example later, but it makes sense that if you were a million times more likely to meet a human than a Martian, but a thousand times less likely to find a human with antennae, then having a final result (posterior) of about a thousand to one sounds right.

The answer you get does depend on the prior. You might have started out with even less belief in the possibility of Martians landing, perhaps 1 in a billion, in which case even after seeing the antennae you would still think it a million times more likely that the person is human, but that is different from the initial thousand to one posterior. We'll see further examples of this later in the chapter.

If we return once again to the 'job of statistics' diagram (Fig. 7.3), we can see that Bayesian inference is doing the same thing as other forms of statistics, taking the sample, or measurement of the real world, which includes many random effects, and then turning this round to learn things about the real world.

The difference in Bayesian inference is that it also asks for a precise prior probability distribution, what you would have thought was likely to be true of the real world before you saw the evidence of the sample measurements. This prior is combined with the same conditional probability (likelihood) used in traditional statistics, but because of the extra 'information' the result is a precise posterior distribution. According to the reasoning, this posterior says how likely it is that particular parameters of the real world have specific values, assuming the prior.

In specific circumstances, the process is mathematically accurate. For example, imagine we are looking at cancer diagnosis. We know the prevalence of a certain cancer in people of the patient's age to be 1 in 1001 and we run a diagnosis that is always positive if you have the disease, but also has a 1 in 1000 chance of being positive if you don't. If the test is positive, Bayesian analysis says that, based on the evidence, the person has exactly a 1 in 2 chance of having the cancer. In this example, the posterior probability is both precise and accurate.

In general, if you have an absolutely accurate idea of the prior probability, then Bayesian analysis does give you a far more precise answer than traditional statistics, but this depends critically on you being able to provide that initial precise prior and for that to be meaningful. This is very important. If you do not have strong grounds for the prior, as is usually the case in Bayesian statistics, you are dealing with quantified belief set in the language of probability, not probabilities themselves. The Bayesian 'machinery' still 'works';[1] however, the result, albeit represented as a probability, is really a *measure of belief*.

7.3   BAYES FOR INTELLIGENT INTERFACES

We are particularly interested in the use of Bayesian methods as an alternative way to do statistics for experiments, surveys and studies. However, Bayesian inference can also be very successfully used within an application to make adaptive or intelligent user interfaces. We'll look at an example of how it could be used to create an adaptive website. In this example there is a clear prior probability distribution and the meaning of the posterior is also clear. I hope the example will solidify the concepts of Bayesian techniques before we look at the slightly more complex case of Bayesian statistical inference.

Figure 7.4 shows the front page of the Isle of Tiree website. There is a menu along the left-hand side; it starts with 'home,' 'about Tiree,' 'accommodation,' and the 12th item is 'sport & leisure.'

Imagine we have gathered extensive data on use by different groups, perhaps by an experiment or perhaps based on real usage data. We find that for most users the likelihood of clicking

---

[1]The numbers you work with follow the same mathematical rules as true probabilities (the Kolomogrov laws [36]), but are not true probabilities in the real world sense. This is a bit like a high school physics demonstration using water flow to simulate electrical current; the water flow follows the same mathematical rules as electricity, but would not light a bulb—*Ceci n'est pas une pipe* [48].

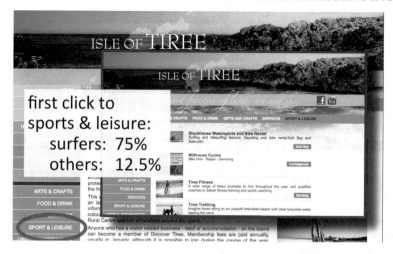

Figure 7.4: Bayesian inference for customisation (source: `https://www.isleoftiree.com/`).

Known visitors stats (*prior*):
        Surfers: 20%; Others: 80%

Imagine 100 visitors to website …
                Surfers   Others
All visitors: 20   80
Click S&L: 15   10

So … if click S&L *posterior* probability
        Surfers: 60%;   Others: 40%

First click to
Sports & Leisure:
        Surfers: 75%
        Others: 12.5%

Figure 7.5: Bayesian inference.

'sport & leisure' as the first selection on the site is 12.5%, but for surfers this figure is 75%. Clearly, different users access the site in different ways, so perhaps we would like to customise the site in some way for different types of users.

Let's imagine we also have figures for the overall proportion of visitors to the site who are surfers or non-surfers, let's say that the figures are 20% surfers, 80% non-surfers. Clearly, as only one in five visitors is a surfer we do not want to make the site too 'surf-centric.'

However, let's look at what we know after the user's first selection (Fig. 7.5).

Consider 100 visitors to the site. On average, 20 of these will be surfers and 80 non-surfers. Of the 20 surfers, on average 75%, that is 15 visitors, are likely to click 'sports & leisure' first.

Of the 80 non-surfers, on average 12.5%, that is 10 visitors, are likely to click 'sports & leisure' first.

So of the 100 visitors, on average 25 in total will click 'sports & leisure' first. Of these, 15 are surfers and 10 non-surfers, that is *if* the visitor has clicked 'sports & leisure' first there is a 60% chance the visitor is a surfer. It therefore becomes more sensible to adapt the site in various ways for these visitors. For visitors who made a different first choice (and hence have a lower chance of being a surfer), we might present the site differently.

This is precisely the kind of reasoning used by advertisers to target marketing and by shopping sites to help make suggestions.

Note here that the prior distribution is given by solid data, as is the likelihood: the premises of Bayesian inference are fully met and thus the results of applying it are mathematically and practically sound.

If you'd like to see how the above reasoning is written mathematically, it goes as follows—using the notation $P(A|B)$ as the conditional probability that A is true given B is true.

likelihood:

P('sports & leisure' first click | surfer) = 0.75

P('sports & leisure' first click | non-surfer) = 0.125

prior:

P(surfer) = 0.2

P(non-surfer) = 0.8

posterior (writing 'S&L' for " 'sports & leisure' first click"):

P(surfer | 'S&L') = P(surfer and 'S&L') / P('S&L')
where:
    P('S&L') = P(surfer and 'S&L') + P(non-surfer and 'S&L')
    P(surfer and 'S&L') = P('S&L' | surfer) * P(surfer)
        = 0.75 * 0.2 = 0.15
    P(non-surfer and 'S&L') = P('S&L' | non-surfer) * P(non-surfer)
        = 0.125 * 0.8 = 0.1

so
    P(surfer | 'S&L') = 0.15 / (0.15 + 0.1) = 0.6

7.3.1   BAYES AS A STATISTICAL METHOD

Bayesian statistics

Let's see how the same principle is applied to statistical inference for a user study result. We assume once again that you are comparing an old system, A, with a new system, B. You are clearly hoping that your newly designed system is better!

Bayesian inference demands that you make precise your prior belief about the outcomes encoded as a probability. Let's say that you have been quite conservative and decided that:

prior probability that A & B are the same: 80%

prior probability that B is better: 20%

You now do a small study with four users, all of whom say they prefer system B. Assuming the users are representative and independent, then this is just like tossing a coin. For the case where A and B are equally preferred, you'd expect an average 50:50 split in preferences, so the chances of seeing all users prefer B is 1 in 16.

The alternative, B better, is a little more complex, as there are usually many ways that something can be more or less better. Bayesian statistics has ways of dealing with this, but for now I'll just assume we have done the groundwork and calculated that the probability of getting all four users to say they prefer B is 3 in 4.

We can now work out a posterior probability based on the same reasoning as we used for the adaptive website. The result of doing this yields the following posterior:

posterior probability that A & B are the same: 25%

posterior probability that B is better: 75%

It is 3x more likely that your new design actually is better :-)

This ratio, 3:1, is called the odds ratio or Bayes factor and there are rules of thumb for determining whether this is deemed good evidence (rather like the 5% or 1% significance levels in standard hypothesis testing). While a 3:1 odds ratio is in the right direction, it would normally be regarded as inconclusive; you would not feel able to draw strong recommendations from this data alone.

BAYES FACTOR AS EVIDENCE

The Bayes factor is used as a sort of 'slot-in' replacement to p-values in hypothesis testing. For a simple H_0 vs. H_1 alternative (e.g., human vs. Martian) the Bayes factor is the ratio of the odds for the two alternatives: P(H_1 | observed data) / P(H_0 | observed data). However, if H_0 vs. H_1 is more complex (e.g., mean = 0 vs. *any other* value), then calculating the Bayes factor involves averaging over the alternative possibilities weighted by the prior probability distribution.

There are common phrases used to describe levels of evidence; the following are due to Kass and Raftery [45] and are widely used.

Bayes factor	Evidence against H_1
1 to 3	Not worth more than a bare mention
3 to 20	Positive
20 to 150	Strong
> 150	Very strong

Also well used are an earlier set of descriptors by Jeffreys [42], which are broadly similar, but offer slightly finer distinctions among the stronger evidence categories.

At first glance, the positive evidence category looks almost dangerously liberal in assigning evidence, compared to the minimum traditional significance level of 5%. However, in practice the averaging behaviour for typical priors includes values close to the null hypothesis, which means the Bayes factor may be more conservative in some cases [75].

Now let's imagine a slightly different prior where you are a little more confident in your new design. You think it four times more likely that you have managed to produce a better design than that you have made no difference (you are still modest enough to admit you may have done it badly!). Codified as a prior probability this gives us:

prior probability that A & B are the same: 20%

prior probability that B is better: 80%

The experimental results are exactly the same, but because the prior beliefs are different the posterior probability distribution is also different:

posterior probability A & B are the same: ~2%

posterior probability B is better: ~98%

The odds ratio is approximately 50:1, which would be considered an overwhelmingly positive result; you would definitely conclude that system B is better.

Here the same study data leads to very different conclusions depending on the prior probability distribution; in other words your prior *belief*. On the one hand, this is a good thing; it precisely captures the difference between tossing the coin you took from your pocket and tossing the one you were given by the showman at the street market. On the other hand, this also shows that the conclusions of Bayesian analysis are highly sensitive to your prior expectations. It is very easy to fall prey to confirmation bias, where the results of the analysis merely rubber stamp your initial impressions.

As is evident, Bayesian inference can be really powerful in a variety of settings. For its use as a statistical tool, however, it is also evident that the choice of prior is a critical issue.

7.4   HOW DO YOU GET THE PRIOR?

Sometimes you have strong knowledge of the prior probability, perhaps based on previous similar experiments. While this is commonly the case when Bayesian inference is used in internal algorithms, it is unlikely to be the case in more typical usability settings such as the comparison between two systems. In the latter you are usually attempting to *quantify your expert judgement*.

Sometimes the evidence from the experiment or study is so overwhelming that it doesn't make much difference what prior you choose ... but in such cases hypothesis testing would give very high significance levels (small p-values), and confidence intervals very narrow ranges. It is nice when this happens, but if this were always the case we would not need the statistics!

Another option is to be conservative in your prior. The first example we gave was very conservative, giving the new system a low probability of success. More commonly, a uniform prior is used, giving everything the same prior probability. This is easy when there are a small number of distinct possibilities, you just make them equal, but it's a little more complex for unbounded value ranges, where often a Cauchy distribution is used ... this is bell shaped, a bit like the Normal distribution, but has fatter edges, like a fried egg with more white.

In fact, if you use a uniform prior then the results of Bayesian statistics are pretty much identical to traditional statistics, the posterior is effectively the likelihood function, and the odds ratio is closely related to the significance level. Indeed in a re-analysis of the data from 855 psychology articles, Wetzels et al. found very little difference in using traditional or Bayesian methods [75].[2]

As we saw, if you do not use a uniform prior, or a prior based on well-founded previous research, you have to be very careful to avoid confirmation bias.

7.5   HANDLING MULTIPLE EVIDENCE

Bayesian methods are particularly good at dealing with multiple *independent* sources of evidence; you simply apply the technique iteratively with the posterior of one study forming the prior to

---

[2]The major differences they found were that default Bayesian factors were slightly more conservative in attributing evidence for the alternative Hypothesis for data with p-values close to 0.05, but slightly more liberal in assigning positive evidence to the null.

the next. It has been suggested that this would be appropriate in HCI [46]. However, you do need to be very careful that the evidence is really independent evidence, or apply corrections if it is not.

Imagine you have applied Bayesian statistics using the task completion times of an experiment to provide evidence that system B is better than system A. You then take the posterior from this study and use it as the prior for applying Bayesian statistics to evidence from an error rate study. If these are really two independent studies this is fine, but if these are the task completion times and error rates from the same study then it is likely that if a participant found the task hard on one system they will have had both slow times and more errors, and vice versa—the evidence is not independent and your final posterior has effectively used some of the same evidence twice!

7.6   INTERNECINE WARFARE

Do be aware that there has been an ongoing, normally good-natured, debate between statisticians on the relative merits of traditional and Bayesian statistics for at least 40 years. While Bayes Rule, the mathematics that underlies Bayesian methods, is applied across all branches of probability and statistics, Bayesian Statistics, the particular use for statistical inference, has always been less well accepted, the Cinderella of statistics.

However, algorithmic uses of Bayesian methods in machine learning and AI have blossomed over recent years, and are widely accepted and regarded across all communities.

CHAPTER 8

Common issues

In this chapter, we will look at some of the issues that are common to the different statistical techniques we have been looking at. It is a mixed bag of potential dangers and positive techniques.

We will start with common dangers. Traditional statistics and Bayesian methods have their own specific pitfalls to avoid: for example interpretation of non-significant as 'no effect' in traditional stats, and confirmation bias for Bayesian stats. They also have some potential pitfalls in common. Perhaps the worst is cherry picking—doing analysis using different tests, and statistics, and methods until you find one that 'works'! You also have to be careful of inter-related factors such as the age and experience of users. By being aware of these dangers you can hope to avoid them!

We then look at two difficult issues: how all the statistics we calculate are themselves random and how to work out what it means to be 'the same but worse.' Finally, we take a more positive turn, looking at the way simulation and empirical methods can be used to calculate statistics of even complex phenomena, and how, despite all of the warnings about misinterpreting probabilities in the past two chapters, there are some strong statements can be made if you look at your whole career rather than just single studies or experiments.

8.1 CHERRY PICKING

Some of the most frequent problems in statistics are forms of cherry picking. This is when you deliberately or accidentally ignore results that for some reason are not to your liking and instead just report those that are advantageous. Focusing on these few cherry picked results may cause you to falsely believe something is true, or inadvertently to mislead your colleagues. We'll look at some of the ways cherry picking occurs, and then at why this is not only bad for your own work, but for the discipline as a whole.

8.1.1 MULTIPLE TESTS

The most obvious form of cherry picking is when you perform multiple tests on lots and lots of things, but only report the successful ones. Perhaps you pick out the few tests that show some effect (p-value or odds ratio) and ignore the rest; or, even worse, you select the few that show the effect you *want* and ignore the ones that point the opposite way!

A classic example of this is when you have a questionnaire administered after a user test. You have 40 questions comparing two versions of a system (A and B) in terms of satisfaction, and the questions cover different aspects of the system and different forms of emotional response. Most of the questions come out mixed between the two systems, but three questions seem to show a marked preference for the new system. You then test these using hypothesis testing and find that all three are statistically significant at 5% level. You report these and feel you have good evidence that system B is better.

But wait a minute, remember that the meaning of the 5% significance level is that there is a 1 in 20 chance of seeing the effect by sheer chance. So, if you have 40 questions and there is no real difference, then you might expect to see, on average, two hits at this 1 in 20 level, sometimes just one, sometimes three or more. In fact, there is an approximately 1 in 3 chance that you will have three or more apparently '5% significant' results with 40 questions.

The answer to this is that if you would have been satisfied with a 5% significance level for a single test, and you have 10 tests, then any single one needs to be at the 0.5% significance level (5% / 10) in order to correct for the multiple tests. If you have 40 questions, this means we should look for 0.125% or $p < 0.00125$.

This method of dividing the target p level by the number of tests is called the Bonferroni correction. It is slightly conservative and there are more exact versions, but for most purposes this version is sufficiently accurate.

When you are reading a report or article that cites statistical significance, but where it appears that there has been no correction, you can adjust for this without recalculating all of their statistics. As a rule of thumb, work out how many significant results you would expect to see and if the number you actually see is a lot more than this you can be pretty confident that at least some of these are real effects.

For example, suppose an article refers to 10 tests and it has calculated that some are significant at the 5% level. On average you'd expect to see one of these 10 at this level by random chance about 50% of the time (remember 5% significance happens by chance one time in twenty). So if there is just one test at 5% significance that is hardly surprising. However, if three or more are at this level, then it seems likely that at least some of these are real effects, as the chances of seeing three or more are quite low (about 1 in 100).

These techniques are sometimes called multiplicity adjustments or multiplicity control.

Bayesian statistics have effectively identical issues. An easy adjustment, rather like the Bonferroni correction, is to simply divide the likelihood of the priors by the number of tests. For example, suppose you have 10 potential interface changes and want to see if they improve the user experience. Perhaps when you consider each individual interface change you are reasonably sure it is an improvement, so you might assign a prior probability of 1/3 for it making an improvement and 2/3 for no improvement. To adjust for the fact that you are trying 10 things, you can simply divide this 1 in 3 prior probability by 10, so your prior for each interface change becomes 1/30 for it being improvement.

As with Bonferroni, this simple adjustment may be a little conservative, and more complex alternatives have been proposed. For example, Gou and Heitjan [35] suggest adjusting the different tests by different amounts to reflect some form of ordering.

Do beware: some writers suggest that this form of correction is not necessary for Bayesian statistics; this is **not true**. If you are in any doubt, look at the randomly generated data in Section 8.3 later in this chapter. Even when there is no effect, by random chance the Bayesian posterior probabilities occasionally suggest there is one.

8.1.2   MULTIPLE STATISTICS

A slightly less obvious form of cherry picking is when you try *different kinds of statistical technique*. First you try a non-parametric test, then a t-test, then a Bayesian test, etc., until something comes out right.

I once saw a paper where all the statistics were using traditional hypothesis testing, and then in the middle there was one test that used Bayesian statistics. There was no explanation and my best bet was that the hypothesis testing had come out negative so they had a go with a Bayesian statistics test and it 'worked.'

This use of multiple kinds of statistics is not usually quite as bad as testing lots of different things, as it is the same underlying data and so the tests are not independent, but if you decide to change the technique you are using mid-analysis, you need to be very clear *why* you are doing it.

It may be that you have realised that you were initially using the wrong test; for example, you might have initially used a test, such as Student's t-test, that assumes Normally distributed data, and realised only after starting the analysis that the data had a different distribution. However, simply swapping statistics partway through in the hope that 'something will come out' is just a form of fishing expedition.

For Bayesian stats the choice of prior can also be a form of cherry picking, if you try one and then another until you get the result you want.

8.1.3   OUTLIERS

Unexpectedly extreme values in your data are called outliers. They may be due to a fault in equipment, or some other irrelevant effect, or may simply occur by chance. If they do appear to be valid data points that just happen to be extreme, you may just let them be, as they are part of the random nature of the phenomenon you are studying. However, even a few outliers can have a disproportionate effect on some statistics, notably arithmetic mean and variance, and so there are arguments that, for some purposes, one gets better results by removing the most extreme outliers.

However, this can introduce the potential for more cherry picking. One of the effects of removing outliers is to reduce the variance of the sample. A large sample variance reduces the likelihood of getting a statistically significant effect, so removing outliers might make stats that were non-significant suddenly fall into the significant range. This then leads to the temptation to strip out outliers until the stats come out 'right.'

Ideally, you should choose a strategy for dealing with outliers *before* you do your analysis. For example, some analysts choose to remove all data that lies more than 2 or 3 standard deviations from the mean. However, there are times when you don't realise outliers are likely to be a problem until they occur. When this happens you should attempt to be as blind to the stats as possible as you choose which outliers to remove. Do avoid removing a few, re-testing, removing a few more and then re-testing again!

8.1.4 POST-HOC HYPOTHESIS

The final kind of cherry picking to beware of is post-hoc hypothesis testing.

You gather your data, visualise it (good practice), notice an interesting pattern, perhaps a correlation between variables, and then test for it.

This is a bit like doing multiple tests, but with an unspecified number of alternative tests. For example, if you have 40 questions in a survey, then there are 780 different possible correlations, so if you happen to notice one and only test for it, this is a bit like doing 780 tests and ignoring 779 of them!

Arguably one should never deviate from one's starting hypothesis. An idealised scientist decides on one or more hypotheses, designs an experiment to test them, and then performs the statistical tests only on the predetermined hypotheses. Apparent patterns in the results that were not part of the original hypotheses cannot be published; they may only be used to help seed hypotheses for future studies.

In practice, this ideal may not be possible, nor even desirable. For example, if you were studying rock retrieved from an asteroid it would be foolish to eschew further analysis and merely set hypotheses for a future space mission. Similarly, if you are analysing the past three years of user logs, you cannot ignore any emergent patterns and simply say "I'll wait another three years." In such cases one can at best be honest and, where possible, attempt to assess potential impact (see Section 8.4.4 below).

8.1.5 THE FILE DRAWER EFFECT

One consequence of cherry picking is that for every positive result published there may be many more negative (non-significant) results that are never published; this is called the file drawer effect. If this is the case then the publications we see may simply be the effects of random chance, not solid results. Such selective publishing may be a deliberate attempt to deceive, but more often it is simply a combination of ignorance and bias. Furthermore, journal reviewing practices typically make it hard or impossible to publish non-significant results. In hypothesis testing the impact of this selective publishing is sometimes called 'p-hacking,' but the file drawer effect can equally be a problem for Bayesian statistics and confidence intervals.

One of the ways to deal with this is to pre-register experiments, including a statement of what hypothesis you wish to test and which statistical technique you plan to use. This makes post-hoc hypotheses very obvious as they were not in the original pre-registration; the author is then forced to justify the reasons for the fresh hypothesis and any mitigation used. If a researcher repeatedly registers experiments, but only publishes the results of a few, this can be used to calibrate the confidence you should have in the few that are published. Pre-registration has become standard practice in many areas of science, and there are proposals to adopt it more widely in human—computer interaction [13].

8.2   INTER-RELATED FACTORS

Another potential danger is where the factors you are trying to control or measure are in some way inter-related, making it hard to interpret results, especially potential causes for observed effects.

8.2.1   NON-INDEPENDENTLY CONTROLLABLE FACTORS

Sometimes you cannot change one parameter without changing others as well. For example, if you are studying diet and you try to reduce sugar intake, then it is likely that either fat intake will go up to compensate or overall calorie intake will fall. You can't reduce sugar without something else changing.

This is a particular problem with user interface properties or features. For example, imagine you find people are getting confused by the underline option on a menu; you might change it so that the menu item says 'underline' when the text is not underlined, and 'remove underline' when it is already underlined. This might improve the underline feature, but then maybe users would become confused because it still says 'italic' when the selected text is already italicised. In practice, once you change one thing, you need to change many others to make a coherent design.

A similar issue occurs if you are trying to implement a general policy or principle, such as interface transparency vs. intelligence. You cannot simply make very small variations on an otherwise identical system.

Because of these inter-relations, in the diet example you cannot simply say, "reducing sugar has this effect;" instead it is more likely to be "reducing sugar whilst keeping the rest of the diet fixed (and hence reducing calories) …" or "reducing sugar whilst keeping calorie intake constant (and hence probably increasing fat) …."

In the menu example, you would not be able to compare only the effects of the underline/remove underline menu options without changing all the menu items, so what you will actually be studying is constant name vs. state-based action naming, or something like that. However, it is also unlikely that you can study constant name vs. state-based action naming in menus without altering all sorts of other aspects of the system as well.

8.2.2   CORRELATED FEATURES

A similar problem can occur when there are features of your users that you cannot directly control at all.

Let's start again with a dietary example. Imagine you have clinical measures of health, perhaps cardiovascular test results, and you want to work out which factors of day-to-day life contribute to health. You decide to administer a lifestyle questionnaire to some patients. One question is about the amount of exercise they take and you find this correlates positively with cardiovascular health; this looks as though you have found something valuable. However, it may be that someone who is a little overweight is less likely to take exercise, or vice versa. The different lifestyle traits, healthy diet, weight, and exercise, are likely to be correlated and thus it can be difficult to disentangle which are the causal factors for measured effects.

In a user interface setting we might have found that more senior managers work best with slightly larger fonts than their juniors. We surmise that this might be something to do with the high level of multi-tasking they do, and the need for 'at a glance' information. However, on the whole those in more senior positions tend to be older than those in more junior positions, so that the preference may simply be related to age-related eyesight problems.

8.3   EVERYTHING IS RANDOM

Table 8.1 shows a selection from a simulated set of 1000 experiments (full data available from the book website). Each 'experiment' uses 20 values generated from a Normal distribution, with mean zero and standard deviation of 1. In a real experiment, of course, we do not know these values, but have to estimate them from the data we gather. The second and third columns show precisely this: for each experiment the calculated mean and standard deviation. Note how these vary, less than a single value would, but still quite substantially. We know the mean is really zero, but the minimum and maximum over all 1000 experiments were -0.6408 and 0.7552, respectively. The estimated standard deviation also varies considerably around its known value of 1.0.

You will not find this too surprising if you did your own experiments in Chapter 2. However, even those who are used to the odd effects of randomness may forget that the same variability is found in more complex statistics such as the p-value used for testing. The fourth column shows the p-value calculated using the Student's T distribution against the null hypothesis that the mean is zero (which it is), and the fifth column has the standard */**/*** annotations representing 5%, 1% and 0.1% significance, respectively ($p < 0.05$, $p < 0.01$, $p < 0.001$). Note how the 8th experiment is the first (of 56) experiments that achieved 5% significance, experiment 82 the first (of 10) with 1%, and experiment 908 even hit 0.1%.

Remember what 5% significance means, a result that should only happen 1 time in 20 if there is no effect (null hypothesis is true). Sure enough, out of 1000 trials 56 were extreme enough to trigger this, around 1 in 20; similarly, 10 out of 1000 for 1% is bang on the average

Table 8.1: Multiple simulated experiments with 20 zero-centred Normally distributed variables per trial (mean (μ) = 0.0, standard deviation (σ) = 1.0), tested against hypothesis that mean=0, and Bayesian comparison of mean=0 vs. mean=1

Experiment #	Mean	Standard Deviation	P-Value		Confidence Interval	Posterior
1	0.32	0.847	0.1093		[-0.08, 0.71]	0.974
2	0.03	1.176	0.9065		[-0.52, 0.58]	1.000
3	0.00	0.716	0.989		[-0.34, 0.33]	1.000
4	0.22	0.785	0.2219		[-0.15, 0.59]	0.996
5	-0.05	0.839	0.7773		[-0.45, 0.34]	1.000
6	-0.20	0.92	0.3533		[-0.63, 0.23]	1.000
7	0.03	1.222	0.918		[-0.54, 0.60]	1.000
8	0.47	0.999	0.049	*	[0.00, 0.94]	0.646
9	0.03	1.056	0.8969		[-0.46, 0.53]	1.000
10	-0.42	0.944	0.0602		[-0.86, 0.02]	1.000
...						
82	-0.51	0.736	0.006	**	[-0.85, -0.16]	1.000
...						
908	0.66	0.751	0.0009	***	[0.31, 1.01]	0.041
...						
996	-0.03	0.897	0.8871		[-0.45, 0.39]	1.000
997	0.15	0.679	0.3288		[-0.17, 0.47]	0.999
998	-0.09	0.717	0.5814		[-0.43, 0.25]	1.000
999	0.11	0.972	0.6098		[-0.34, 0.57]	1.000
1,000	0.19	0.863	0.3449		[-0.22, 0.59]	0.998

one would expect. However, in none of these experiments is there any real effect; just like the experiments with fair coins, every so often something extreme happens by sheer chance.

This randomness extends to other derived statistics including the confidence interval (column 6) and Bayesian posterior probability (column 7). The Bayesian posterior calculated in this table is a simple comparison against an alternative of a mean of 1, with a prior of a mean of zero or one being equally likely (uniform prior); note that the posterior is usually close to 1 (highly likely to be mean of zero), but occasionally drifts quite far including in experiment 908 being 96% certain the mean is 1 rather than zero.

Table 8.2: Multiple simulated experiments with 20 *non-zero-centred* Normally distributed variables per trial (mean $(\mu) = 0.5$, standard deviation $(\sigma) = 1.0$), tested against hypothesis that mean=0, and Bayesian comparison of mean=0 vs. mean=1

Experiment #	Mean	Standard Deviation	P-Value		Confidence Interval	Posterior
1	0.75	1.085	0.006	**	[0.24, 1.26]	0.007
2	0.25	0.681	0.1137		[-0.07, 0.57]	0.993
3	0.40	0.877	0.0555		[-0.01, 0.81]	0.881
4	0.01	0.981	0.9505		[-0.45, 0.47]	1.000
5	0.48	1.061	0.0553		[-0.01, 0.98]	0.578
...						
996	0.48	0.881	0.0245	*	[0.07, 0.89]	0.592
997	0.24	1.311	0.4264		[-0.38, 0.85]	0.995
998	0.65	0.83	0.0023	**	[0.27, 1.04]	0.044
999	0.57	0.778	0.0039	**	[0.21, 0.94]	0.194
1,000	0.15	0.985	0.4973		[-0.31, 0.61]	0.999

Also note I include a column for the experiment number. Recall the discussion of cherry picking (Section 8.1). Without the experiment number, just looking at the selected data rows, you might think that I have provided all of the experiments and so the number of significant experimental results suggests there is actually an effect. Similarly, if I had just presented row 908 and others like it, the Bayesian posteriors would have suggested a true mean of 1 rather than zero.

Table 8.2 shows a selection from another simulated set of 1000 experiments, but this time from data with a Normal distribution with mean 0.5. It is then tested using the null hypothesis of mean zero as in the previous table, and confidence interval and Bayesian posterior are also listed.

Looking first at the p-values and significance test, in 607 of the experiments the p-value was significant at 5%, of which 345 were at 1% and 115 at 0.01%. These are quite prevalent and indeed we know that the null hypothesis (that the mean is zero) really is false. However, we would only conclude this, even at 5% which is quite lax, in less than 2/3 of the experiments. We would clearly need a lot more than 20 trials in an experiment to be able to reliably distinguish this level of difference from zero. This is also evident in the confidence intervals which are quite wide, showing substantial uncertainty. That is, there is a strong potential for a false negative conclusion (known in statistics as a Type II error). In Chapter 10 we will explore in greater

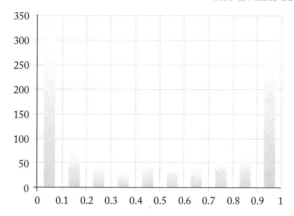

Figure 8.1: Distribution of Bayesian posterior probability over 1000 experiments, starting from a uniform 50:50 prior.

depth how it is possible to increase the statistical power of experiments, that is make them less likely to have false negatives.

Another point to note is that the ratio of "**" to "*" results (345 out of 607) is a lot higher than for the case where there is really no effect (10 out of 56). This is typically the case when there is a real effect and it has been suggested [66] that this p-curve can be used to determine whether researchers have been withholding non-significant results (the file drawer effect) and selectively reporting significant ones, a form of p-hacking.

The Bayesian posterior is again calculated based on the simple decision between a mean of 0 or 1. Given the actual mean is 0.5, the posterior, not surprisingly, varies between the two, although, perhaps more surprisingly, it is rarely in the middle. Figure 8.1 shows the distribution of the posterior over all 1000 experiments; in fact in about 2/3 of the experiments (620 out of 1000) the posterior *appears* to give very strong evidence in one direction or the other (about 50:50 for each), even though the true value is in fact exactly in the middle. This is due to the way the tails of the Normal distribution fall off rapidly, making even small changes in the experimental outcome give rise to large differences in the calculated Bayesian posterior.

To be fair, this is a particularly simplistic Bayesian test (to make it easy to calculate), and exhibits a difficult case where none of the alternatives considered correspond to reality. The main point is that in all kinds of statistics we need to be aware that the calculations are based on our data and are thus subject to noise, random effects and other forms of error. In statistics we are always reasoning through the fog of uncertainty.

10 coin tosses:
Is it a fair coin?

What about ...?

Figure 8.2: Is it a fair coin?

8.4 THE SAME OR WORSE

Many statistical tests depend on the idea of outcomes that are the *same or worse* than the one you have observed. For example, if the difference in response times between two systems is 5.7 sec, then 5.8, 6.0, 23.5 sec are all 'the same or worse,' that is equally or more surprising. We will see that for numeric values this is fairly straightforward, but it can be more complex when looking at other kinds of patterns in data. This is critical when you are making 'post-hoc hypotheses,' noticing some pattern in the data and then trying to verify whether it is a real effect or simple chance.

8.4.1 EVERYTHING IS UNLIKELY

You have got hold of the stallholder's coin and are wondering if it is fair or maybe weighted in some way. Imagine you toss it 10 times (see Fig. 8.2) and get the sequence: THTHHHTTHH. Does that seem reasonable? What about all heads: HHHHHHHHHH?

In fact, if the coin is fair the probability of any sequence of heads and tails is exactly the same: 1 in 1024

$$\text{Prob(THTHHHTTHH)} = 1/2^{10} \sim 0.001$$

$$\text{Prob(HHHHHHHHHH)} = 1/2^{10} \sim 0.001$$

The same would be true of a pack of cards. There are 52! different ways a pack of cards can come out,[1] approximately the number of atoms in our galaxy. Each order is equally likely in a well-shuffled pack, so any pack you pick up is an incredibly unlikely order.

However, this goes against our intuition that some orders of cards, some patterns of coin tosses are more special than others. Surely all heads is more extreme.

This is exactly where we need to have an idea of things that are *similar or equally surprising* to the thing we are observing. For the line of 10 heads, the only thing *equally surprising* would be a line of 10 tails. However for the pattern THTHHHTTHH, with 6 heads and 4 tails in a pretty unsurprising order (not even all the heads together), pretty much any other order is equally or more surprising, indeed if you are thinking about a fair coin, arguably the only thing less surprising is exactly five of each.

---

[1]The notation 52! is the factorial, the product of all the numbers up to 52. That is 52x51x50 ... x3x2x1.

8.4.2   NUMERIC DATA

I said that this idea of 'same or worse' is relatively straightforward for numeric data such as completion time in an experiment, or number of heads in coin tosses.

Let's look at our coin tossing example, focusing on the number of heads; that is we are reducing the complexity of coin tosses in all kinds of orders to the simple numeric statistic of the count of heads. In our example, we got 6 heads out of 10 tosses, so that 6, 7, 8, 9, 10 heads would be equally or more surprising, as would 6, 7, 8, 9, 10 tails.

So ...

prob ('the same or worse') assuming fair
$$
\begin{aligned}
&= && \text{prob (anything but 5H 5T)} \\
&= && 1 - \text{prob (exactly 5 heads)} \\
&= && 1 - 252/1024 \\
&\sim && 75\%
\end{aligned}
$$

As we suspected, the pattern THTHHHTTHH is not particularly surprising after all.

Let's look at another example: say it had been 9 heads and one tail. Now 10 heads, or 9 tails, or 10 tails would all be equally or more surprising. So ...

prob ('the same or worse') assuming fair
$$
\begin{aligned}
&= && \text{prob (9 heads) + prob (10 heads)} \\
& && \qquad\quad + \text{prob (9 tails) + prob (10 tails)} \\
&= && 10/1024 + 1/1024 + 10/1024 + 1/1024 \\
&= && 22/1024 \\
&\sim && 2\%
\end{aligned}
$$

So yes, 9 heads is starting to look more surprising, but is it enough to call the stallholder out for cheating?

As a final example, imagine 90 heads out of 100 tosses—the same proportion, but more tosses, therefore you expect things to 'average out' more. Here the things that are equally or more surprising are 90 or more heads or 90 or more tails.

prob ('the same or worse') assuming fair
$$
\begin{aligned}
&= && \text{prob (nos heads} \le 90) + \text{prob (nos tails} \ge 90) \\
&< && 1 \text{ in a million}
\end{aligned}
$$

The maths for this gets a little more complicated, but turns out to be less than one in a million. If this were a Wild West film this is the point the table would get flung over and the shooting start!

For continuous distributions, such as task completion times, the principle is the same. The maths to work out the probabilities gets harder still, but here you just look up the numbers in a statistical table, or rely on R or SPSS to work it out for you.

For example, you measure the average task completion time for ten users of system A as 117.3 sec, and for ten users of system B it is 98.1 sec. System B was 18.2 sec faster, on average, for the participants in your user test. Can you conclude that your newly designed system B is indeed faster to use?

Just as with the coin tosses, the probability of a precisely 18.2 sec difference is vanishingly small, it could be 18.3 or 18.1, or so many possible values. Indeed, even if the systems were identical, the probabilities of the difference being precisely zero, or 0.1 sec, or 0.2 sec are all still pretty tiny. Instead you look at the probability (given the systems are the same) that the difference is 18.2 or greater.

8.4.3   MORE COMPLEX 'OR WORSE'

For numeric values, the only real complication is whether you want a one-tailed test or a two-tailed test. In the case of checking whether the coin is fair, you would be equally upset if it had been weighted in some way in either direction; hence you look at both sides equally and work out (for the 90 heads out of 100): prob (nos heads $\geq$ 90) + prob (nos tails $\geq$ 90).

However, for the response time, you probably only care about your new system being faster than the old one. So in this case you would only look at the probability of the time difference being $\geq$ 18.2, and not bother about it being larger in the opposite direction.

Things get more complex in various forms of combinatorial data, for example friendship circles in network data. Here what it means to be the 'same or worse' can be far more difficult to decide.

As an example of this kind of complexity, we'll return to playing cards. Recall that there are as many ways to shuffle the pack as atoms in the galaxy. I sometimes play a variety of 'patience' (a solitaire card game) which involves laying out a 7 × 7 grid with the lower left triangle exposed and the upper right face down.

One day I was dealing these out and noticed that three consecutive cards had been Jack of clubs, 10 of clubs, 9 of clubs (Fig. 8.3). My first thought was that I had not shuffled the cards well and this pattern was due to some systematic effects from a previous card game. However, I then realised that the previous game would not lead to sequences of cards in suit. So what was going on? Remembering the raindrops on the Plain of Nali, is this chance or an omen?

Let's look a little more closely. If you deal three cards in a row (Fig. 8.4), what is the probability it will be a decreasing sequence?

Well, the first card can be anything except an ace or a 2, that is 44 out of 52 cards, or 11/13. After this the second and third cards are precisely determined by the first card, so have probability of 1/51 and 1/50, respectively. Overall, the probability of three cards being in a downward run in suit is 11/33350, or about 1 in 3000 ... pretty unlikely and if you were doing statistics after a usability experiment you would get rather excited with $p < 0.001$.

However, that is not the end of the story. I would have been equally surprised if it had been an ascending run, or if the run had been anywhere amongst the visible cards where there

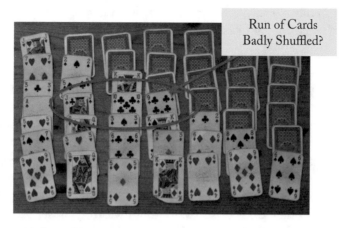

Figure 8.3: A run in clubs—Chance or omen?

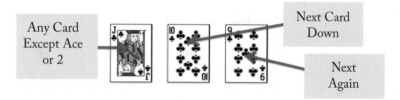

Figure 8.4: Three in a row—How likely?

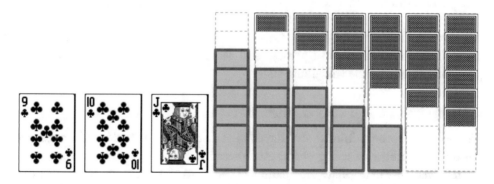

Figure 8.5: Equally surprising: (left) upward run (right) 15 different starting positions.

are 15 possible start positions for a run of three. So, our probability of it being a run up or down in any of these start positions is now 30 x 11 / 33350 or about 1 in a 100.

But then there are also vertical runs up and down the cards, or perhaps runs of the same number from different suits, which would also be equally surprising. Finally, how many times do I play the game? I probably only notice when there is something interesting (cherry picking). Suddenly my run of three does not looks so surprising after all.

8.4.4   POST-HOC CORRECTIONS

In some ways, noticing the Jack, ten, nine run is a bit like a post-hoc hypothesis.

You have run your experiment and looked at the data, and you notice that it looks as though expert response time is slower than novice response time. This looks interesting, so you follow it up with a formal statistical test. You divide the data into novice and expert, calculate averages, do the sums and it comes out significant at 1%. Yay, you have found out something … or have you?

What else would have been equally interesting that you might have noticed: age effects, experience, exposure to other kinds of software, those wearing glasses vs. those with perfect vision? Remember the Bonferroni correction. If there are 10 things that would have been equally surprising, your 1% statistical significance is really only equivalent to 10%, which may be just plain chance.

Think again about the raindrops patterns on the Plain of Nali. One day's rainfall included three drops in an almost straight line, but turned out to be an entirely random fall pattern. You notice the three drops in a line, but how many lots of three are there, how close to a line before you call it straight? Would small triangles or squares have been equally surprising?

In an ideal (scientific) world, you would use patterns you notice in data as hypotheses for a further round of experiments … but often that is not possible and you need to be able to both spot patterns and make tests of their reliability on the same data. One way to ease this is to visualise a portion of the data and then check it on the rest—this is similar to techniques used in machine learning. However, again that may not always be possible.

So, if you do need to make post-hoc hypotheses, try to make an assessment of what other things would be 'similar or more surprising' and use this to help decide whether you are just seeing random patterns in the wild-flung stars.

8.5   SIMULATION AND EMPIRICAL METHODS

We have seen that both traditional and Bayesian statistical methods depend on having some model of the probabilities of seeing events given certain assumptions (the likelihood). In some cases it is relatively easy to calculate the theoretical distribution, such as the probability of having exactly 9 heads out of 10 coin tosses. In others, it is potentially possible, but harder to work out the maths; for example, in the two-horse races it is the number of tosses of the 'losing' side after the winner gets to 10 first. Finally, there are cases that are so complex that there is no closed formula (as in a tractable mathematical description).

In Section 4.2.5 we saw that nonparametric statistics can sometimes be used where the distribution is either unusual or unknown. However, where we do have some understanding of the process and probabilities, nonparametric methods ignore this additional knowledge and thus lose statistical power. Furthermore, nonparametric statistics themselves only apply to particular circumstances; for example, comparing values that can be easily ordered.

In these cases we can sometimes apply simulation or empirical methods. This is where we run some form of computer simulation based on mathematical probabilities or observed data. By running lots of simulations, we can observe the likelihood of the results we have observed. For example, if we ran a two-horse race and the losing side had just two coins, we could run lots and lots of simulations of two-horse races and look at the proportion where the loser has two or fewer coins. The artificial data in Section 8.3 is an example of this.

As an example of this, I was once at a university marking meeting where students had been divided into groups (let's say 10 groups of 10 students each) and pairs of tutors had marked the talks of all the students from each group. One group seemed to have a much higher average mark than the others. The question was whether this was just random chance (that group just happened to have stronger students), or whether its markers were more generous than those for the other groups. By now you will realise how easy it is to think there is some sort of systematic effect, when it is just random chance!

Extreme statistics (that is measures such as maximum and minimum) have quite complex mathematics, so while it is possible to work out the likelihood of the observed marks, it would be quite difficult. However, during the meeting one of the staff present created a simple simulation where each mark was assumed to be Normally distributed. The simulation calculated 100 random marks, and then looked at the maximum and minimum group mark. This was repeated lots of times and the simulated maxima and minima were typically further apart than the ones we'd actually seen (and wrongly suspected might be unusually spread out).

In this case it is quite common to assume marks are Normally distributed. Of course sometimes student data is not like this, and we might suspect that it is bimodal, with semi-separate groups of stronger and weaker students. If so, rather than a simulation based on the Normal distribution we could have used one based on empirical data: take the actual 100 marks of the students, randomly place them into groups of 10 and then look at the averages of the simulated groups.

These simulation techniques are particularly useful where the system we are observing is particularly complex (for example traffic flows in a town), or where we know that the theoretical distribution is in some way hard to deal with (such as Power-law data from social networks).

8.6   WHAT YOU CAN SAY—PHENOMENA AND STATISTICIANS

The descriptions of significance testing and confidence intervals in Chapter 6 included a lot of warnings about what is not true. Similarly, for Bayesian statistics in Chapter 7 we saw that the 'probabilities' it generates are usually just measures of belief. It sounds as if you can't know anything really, and there is some truth in this; in statistics we are peering into the unknown! However, there are things that you can say with certainty about all of these.

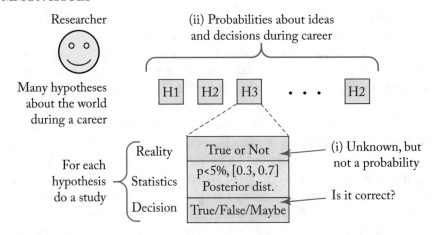

Figure 8.6: Probabilities of individual hypotheses vs. decisions during a career.

To think about this more clearly you should consider not just a single experiment or study, but all the studies an individual or laboratory has performed over a number of years. Figure 8.6 shows an individual researcher with many hypotheses about the world throughout their career, just like you. Each hypothesis is a fact about the world, it is either true or not. The truth of the hypothesis is unknown, but there are no probabilities. Statistics are used to make some sort of assessment of the truth of the hypothesis, or perhaps estimate unknown values. These *estimates* or *assessments* are probabilistic, as we have seen (Section 8.3), and therefore it is possible to make strong probability statements about the ideas and decisions of the researcher throughout their career.

If you run experiments or studies, and you calculate the 95% confidence interval for each and then work on the assumption that the real value lies in that range, then, throughout your career, at least 95% of the time you will be right.

Similarly, if you calculate 99% confidence intervals (usually much wider) and work on the assumption that the real value lies in that range, then, throughout your career, at least 99% of the time you will be right.

This is not to say that for any given experiment the probability of the real value lies in the range, it either does or it doesn't. Rather, it puts a limit on the probability that you are wrong if you make that assumption. These two statements sound almost the same, but the former is about the real value of something that may have no probability associated with it, it is just unknown; the latter is about the fact that you do lots of experiments, each effectively like the toss of a coin.

So if you assume something is in the 95% confidence interval, you really can be 95% confident that you are right.

Similarly, when you create a prior distribution in Bayesian statistics, this can be best thought of as an estimate of probability about you, as a designer, researcher, or statistician, rather than about the phenomenon itself.

This is easiest to envisage when using Bayesian statistics as an alternative to hypothesis testing. Imagine you have created a new interface technique. If three out of four of the ideas you have for new interfaces turn out to be good ones, then it would be reasonable to assign a prior probability of 0.75 for the improved version being better vs. 0.25 for it being no better than the old one. In contrast, if you are not such a good designer and only one in ten of your ideas work out well, then a prior of 0.1 for improvement and 0.9 for no improvement would be called for. The prior is an estimate of your ideas *as a designer*, not each design.

Of course, this is about *all* of the experiments that you or others do. However, often only positive results are published, so it is *not* necessarily true of the whole published literature (as we saw in Section 8.1.5). We will return to these issues in greater detail in Section 11.6.

CHAPTER 9

Differences and distinctions

9.1 PHILOSOPHICAL DIFFERENCES

Although they are both founded in probability theory, traditional statistics and Bayesian statistics have fundamental philosophical differences in the way they treat uncertainty. Bayesian methods demand that uncertainty is quantified, whereas traditional methods accept the uncertainty and reason from that position. However, in practice our knowledge is somewhere between complete ignorance and precise probability, and both methods have ways of dealing with this in-between knowledge.

9.1.1 WHAT DO WE KNOW ABOUT THE WORLD?

We have seen that both traditional statistics and Bayesian statistics effectively start with the same underlying data, and in many circumstances yield effectively equivalent results. However, they adopt fundamentally different philosophical stances in the way they use that data to answer questions about the world. These philosophical differences are critical in interpreting their results.

Traditional statistics effectively assumes nothing about the world: are there Martians or not? Is your new design better than the old one or not? It is not so much neutral as taking no sides at all. It then seeks to reason from that state of unknowledge.

Bayesian statistics instead asks you to quantify that unknowledge into prior probabilities, and then reasons in an apparently mathematically clean way, but based on those guesstimates.

In some ways traditional statistics is post-modern, accepting uncertainty and, even in the eventual interpretation of the results, allowing it to remain. In contrast, Bayesian statistics suggests a more closed world, that is one where we know everything and there are no external factors. However, with Bayesian statistics the uncertainty is still there, it is just encapsulated in the guesstimate of the prior.

We can summarise these different philosophical stances about our knowledge of the world as:

> *traditional statistics*
> – assume nothing
> – reason from unknowledge
> *Bayesian statistics*
> – assume precise 'prior' probabilities

– reason mathematically from guesstimates

9.1.2   NOT SO DIFFERENT

So, on the surface they have radically different assumptions about the unknown features of the real world. Traditional statistics assumes no knowledge of the real value, and Bayesian statistics assumes a precise probability distribution. However, neither the world, nor the statistics we use to make sense of it, are as clear-cut as that.

Usually we have some knowledge about the likelihood (in the day-to-day sense) of things: you are pretty unlikely to encounter Martians; the coin you've pulled from your pocket is likely to be fair; that new design for the software, which you've put a lot of effort into creating, should be better than the old system. However, typically we *do not have a precise measure of that knowledge.*

In their purest form, traditional statistics *entirely ignores that knowledge* and Bayesian statistics asks you to *make it precise* in a way that goes beyond your actual knowledge, turning uncertainty into precise probability. The former ignores information, the latter forces you to invent it! In practice, both techniques are a little more nuanced.

In traditional statistics the significance level you are willing to accept as good evidence ($p < 5\%$, $p < 1\%$) often reflects your prior beliefs: you will probably need a very high level before you really call the Men in Black, or even accept that the coin may be loaded. Effectively there is a level of Bayesian reasoning applied during interpretation.

Similarly, while Bayesian statistics demands a precise prior probability distribution, in practice often uniform or other forms of very 'spread' priors are used, reflecting the high degree of uncertainty. Ideally, it would be good to try a number of priors to obtain a form of sensitivity analysis, rather as we did in the example in Chapter 7, Section 7.3.1, but I have not seen this done in practice, possibly because it would add another level of interpretation to explain!

9.2   SO WHICH IS IT?

This is the point where I nail my colours to the mast—should you use traditional statistics or Bayesian methods? With all the controversy in the media about the 'statistical crisis,' should one opt for alt-stats or stay with conservative ones? Of course the answer will partly be 'it depends,' but for most purposes I think there is a best answer …

9.2.1   THE STATISTICAL CRISIS

You may have seen stories about the 'statistical crisis' [3]. A variety of papers and articles in the technical and sometimes even popular press have highlighted general poor statistical practice. This has touched many disciplines, including HCI [8, 46].

Some have focused on the 'replication crisis,' the fact that many attempts to repeat scientific studies have failed to reproduce the original (often statistically significant) outcomes. Others have focused on the statistics itself, especially p-hacking, where wittingly or unwittingly scientists use various means to ensure they get the necessary $p < 5\%$ to enable them to publish their results.

Some of these problems are intrinsic to the scientific publishing process.

First, the tendency for journals only to accept positive results, so that non-significant results do not get published—the file drawer effect. This sounds reasonable until you remember that the $p < 5\%$ means that even if there is really no effect at all, on average one time in twenty the measurements mean that you reject the null hypothesis (appear to have a positive finding) by sheer chance. So if 100 scientists do experiments where there is no real effect, typically this will lead to 5 apparently 'publishable' effects.

Secondly, the 'publish or perish' culture of academia means that researchers may 'bend' the facts slightly to get publishable results. To be fair this may be because they are convinced for other reasons that something is true, so they 'gild the lily' a little, ignoring negative indications and emphasising positive ones. As we saw previously, famous scientists have done this in the past, and, because what they did happened to be true, history has overlooked the poor stats (or looked the other way).

Weirdly, however, 'publish or perish' culture may act to reduce the file drawer effect. Because researchers know that they can only publish statistically significant results, they deliberately opt for uninteresting research: experiments and studies examining hypotheses that they are pretty certain will yield significant results.

One could imagine a publishing system where acceptance was focused on asking good questions and applying sound methodology, rather than whether the results happened to come out well. In the case of pre-registration of experiments, this might mean accepting papers for publication based on the registration, irrespective of results. This would avoid many potential p-hacking and similar problems, and lead to more adventurous and exciting research. However, it is unlikely to happen soon.

Most of the publicity on the so-called statistical 'crisis' has focused on traditional hypothesis testing. However, the potential problems in traditional statistics have been well known for at least 40 years and are largely connected with poor use or poor interpretation, rather than intrinsic weaknesses in the statistical techniques themselves. Furthermore, most of the problems apply equally to all kinds of statistical method.

There have been some changes in the culture, which may have led to the current level of publicity. One is the increasing publication pressures mentioned above. Another is that in years gone by when scientists needed to do statistics they would typically ask a statistician for advice, especially if their work was at all unusual or unlike previous studies. Indeed, my own first job was at an agricultural engineering research institute, where, in addition to my main role doing mathematical and computational modelling, I was part of the Institute's statistics advisory team. Nowadays, time and budgetary constraints mean that universities and research institutions are less likely to offer easy access to statistical advice, so instead researchers reach for easy to use, but potentially easy to misuse, statistical packages.

However, it is worth noting that there is also a certain amount of hype amidst the genuine concern about the 'crisis,' including some fairly shaky statistical methods in some of the papers that criticise statistical methods!

9.2.2 ALTERNATIVE STATISTICS

As noted, most of the 'bad press' has focused on traditional statistics and the well-understood issues that arise when they are used inexpertly or badly. However, when used properly, traditional statistics (both hypothesis testing and confidence intervals) tend to be relatively conservative.

Nevertheless, the reaction in some quarters to this 'crisis' has been to abandon statistics entirely; famously (or perhaps infamously) the journal *Basic and Applied Social Psychology* has banned all hypothesis testing [80]. However, this is a bit like getting worried about the safety of a cruise ship sinking and so jumping into the water to avoid drowning. The answer to poor statistics is better statistics, not no statistics!

Others have reacted by looking toward alternative statistics or 'new statistics,' including both traditional confidence intervals and Bayesian statistics. Some of this thinking is quite valid: good use of statistics includes using the correct type of analysis for the kinds of data and information you have available. Furthermore, many traditional methods and tests exist because they were easy to calculate in the days before cheap and powerful computers. However, the advocacy of these alternatives can sometimes include an element of snake oil (and paper titles such as "*Using Bayes to get the most out of non-significant results*" probably don't help [16]).

Crucially, most of the problems that have been identified in the 'statistical crisis' also apply to alternative methods: selective publication, p-hacking (or various other forms of cherry picking), post-hoc hypotheses. In addition, reduced familiarity can lead to poorer statistical execution and reporting. Bayesian statistics in particular currently requires considerable expertise to be used correctly. Indeed, at the time of writing the Wikipedia page for Bayes Factor (Bayesian alternative to hypothesis testing) includes, as its central example, precisely this kind of inexpert use of the methods [76].

There are good reasons why, even after more than 40 years of debate, most professional statisticians still use traditional methods!

9.3 ON BALANCE (MY ADVICE)

Based on all these factors my personal advice is: for most things stick with traditional statistics. This is partly because, despite the potential misuse, there is still better general understanding of these methods and their pitfalls. You are more likely to do them right and your readers are more likely to have an idea of what they mean.

However, do, where possible, *always quote confidence intervals* alongside any form of p-value (APA also recommend this [2]). Also, always be careful to include in the text of your papers, or in supporting online material, *all the data necessary to recreate your statistics*, at the very least all means, variances, numbers of subjects, etc., but if possible your full (anonymised) data.

This will enable others to cross-check your results and use them in subsequent meta-analysis (see Chapter 11, Section 11.6).

This said, there are a number of circumstances when using Bayesian statistics is not only a good idea, but the only sensible thing to do. These are usually circumstances where you know the prior and are involved in some sort of decision-making. For example, when a patient is being tested for a medical condition, doctors know the underlying prevalence of various diseases, so they should use this knowledge as part of diagnostic reasoning. This also applies to the algorithmic use of Bayesian methods in intelligent or adaptive interfaces.

If you do choose to use Bayesian statistics, you need to ensure that you consult an expert, especially if you are dealing with continuous values (such as completion times), as the theory around these is particularly complex (as is evident on the Wikipedia page!). Do be careful that your prior is not simply confirming your own bias. Also be aware that the odds ratios that are taken as acceptable evidence seem (to a traditional statistician) to be somewhat lax (and 5% sig. is already quite lax), so I would advise using one of the stricter levels. This advice may of course change as our familiarity with different methods grows, or as tools adapt to embody more knowledge and 'just in time' assistance.

One of the strengths of Bayesian statistics is that it tends to make one think toward degrees of evidence rather than the sharp 'has it passed the line' of the 5% significance level. That is not to say that more binary distinctions are absent from Bayesian statistics, and there are value ranges of the Bayes factor[1] with descriptive terms such as 'strong,' or 'very strong,' which are used in a similar way to '$p < 5\%$' or '$p < 1\%$' (see Chapter 7, Section 7.3.1).

Conversely, traditional statistics can also be used in much more nuanced ways. Recall that one of the main reasons for the simplistic binary distinction of statistical hypothesis testing (significant vs. non-significant) stems from the days when *computation* was performed by hand. Converting a statistical value, such as that from a t-test, into a p-value was a very lengthy process. Fixed levels such as 5%, 1%, and 0.1% could be pre-computed and then the value from a specific table looked up against the pre-computed tables. In a digital age when it is possible to quote the precise value of p at, say 0.0136, the old 'is it, isn't it' approach to testing is no longer necessary.

In early 2019 a special issue of *Nature* was dedicated to just these changes. The editorial suggests that science should retain traditional statistical methods, but entirely ditch terms such as 'statistically significant' and 'non-significant' and instead rely solely on quoting specific p-values [74]. The American Statistical Association (ASA) *Statement on p-Values* [73] stops a little short of banning the terms, but makes strong warnings against dichotomous readings of hypothesis testing.

In the coming years we may well move to a point where the more objective techniques of traditional statistics are retained, but some of the lessons of Bayesian approaches are incorporated into them.

---

[1]The language used is slightly different, but this is basically the ratio of the likelihoods of H_1 and H_0.

9.4 FOR BOTH

Whether you use traditional statistics, p-values, confidence intervals, Bayesian statistics, or tea-leaf reading—make sure you use the statistics properly. *Understand what you are doing* and *what the results you are presenting mean.*

     … and I hope this book helps!

9.5 ENDNOTE

For a balanced view of Bayesian methods see the interview with Peter Diggle, President of the Royal Statistical Society [64]. However, it is perhaps telling that the Royal Statistical Society's own mini-guide for non-statisticians, *Making Sense of Statistics*, avoids mentioning Bayesian methods entirely [65].

PART III

Design and Interpretation

CHAPTER 10

Gaining power – the dreaded 'too few participants'

10.1 IF THERE IS SOMETHING THERE, MAKE SURE YOU FIND IT

Statistical power is about whether an experiment or study is likely to *reveal an effect if it is present*. Without a sufficiently 'powerful' study, you risk being in the middle ground of 'not proven,' not being able to make a strong statement either for or against whatever effect, system, or theory you are testing.

You've recruited your participants and run your experiments or posted an online survey and gathered your responses; you put the data into SPSS and ... "not significant" (Fig. 10.1). Six months' work wasted and your plans for your funded project or Ph.D. shot to ruins.

So, how do you avoid the dread "n.s."?

Part of the job of statistics is to make sure you don't say anything that is wrong, to ensure that when you say something is true, there is good evidence that it really is. This is why, in traditional hypothesis testing statistics, you have a high bar to reject the null hypothesis. Typically, the alternative hypothesis is the thing you are really hoping will be true, but you only declare it likely to be true if you are convinced that the null hypothesis is very unlikely. Bayesian statistics has slightly different kinds of criteria, but the ultimate purpose is the same, to ensure you don't have false positives.

However, you can have the opposite problem, false negatives—there may be a real effect there, but your experiment or study is simply not sensitive enough to detect it. Statistical power[1] is all about avoiding these false negatives.

The standard way to increase statistical power is simply to recruit more participants. No matter how small the effect, if you have a sufficiently large sample, you are likely to detect it ... but 'sufficiently large' may be many, many people.

In HCI studies the greatest problem is often finding sufficient participants to do meaningful statistics. For professional practice we hear that 'five users are enough.' However, as we discussed in Section 1.4.3, this figure was based on particular historical contingencies and in the context of single formative evaluations during an iterative development process. It was never intended for summative evaluations and certainly not for studies where statistical analyses are

---

[1]Note the use of the term 'power' here is not the same as when we talk about power-law distributions for network data. See Section 4.2.4.

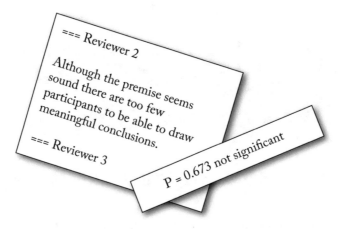

Figure 10.1: Don't you hate it when ….

needed. This said, even obtaining 12 or 20 participants per condition (two arbitrary rules of thumb I've heard quoted) is a challenge.

Happily, increasing the number of participants is not the only way to increase power. In this chapter, we will see that power arises from a combination of:

- the size of the effect you are trying to detect,

- the size of the study (number of trials/participants), and

- the size of the 'noise' (the random or uncontrolled factors).

We will discuss various ways in which careful design and selection of subjects and tasks can increase the power of your study, albeit sometimes requiring care in interpreting results. For example, we will see that using a very narrow user group can reduce individual differences in knowledge and skill (reduce noise) and make it easier to see the effect of a novel interaction technique, but it also reduces the validity for generalisation beyond that group. In another example, we will also see how careful choice of a task can even be used to deal with infrequent expert slips.

Often these techniques *sacrifice generality*, so you need to understand how your choices have affected your results and be prepared to explain this in your reporting: with great (statistical) power comes great responsibility!

Nevertheless, if a restricted experiment or study has shown some effect, at least you have results to report, and then, if the results are sufficiently promising, you can go on to do further targeted experiments or larger-scale studies, knowing that you are not on a wild goose chase.

10.2   THE NOISE–EFFECT–NUMBER TRIANGLE

At the heart of gaining power in your studies is understanding the noise–effect–number triangle. We said that power arises from a combination of the size of the effect you are trying to detect, the *size of the study* (number of trials/participants) and the *size of the 'noise'* (the random or uncontrolled factors). We can increase power by addressing any one of these.

Cast your mind back to your first statistics course, or when you first opened a book on statistics.

The standard deviation (s.d., σ) is one of the most common ways to measure the variability of a data point. This variability is often due to 'noise,' or the things you can't control or measure.

For example, the average adult male height in the UK is about 5 ft 9 in. with a standard deviation of about 3 in. (7.5 cm); most British men are between 5 ft 6 in. (165 cm) and 6 ft (180 cm) tall.

However, if you take a random sample and look at the average (arithmetic mean), this average varies less, as typically your sample has some people taller than average, and some people shorter than average, and they tend to cancel out. The variability of the average is called the standard error of the mean (or just s.e.), and is often drawn as little 'error bars' on graphs or histograms, to give you some idea of the accuracy of the average measure.

You might also remember that, for many kinds of data, the standard error of the mean is given by:

$$s.e. = \sigma/\sqrt{n} \quad \text{(or, if } \sigma \text{ is an estimate, } \sqrt{(n-1)})$$

In the height example, if the standard deviation of male heights is 3 in., the standard error of the mean of 100 heights is 0.3 in. (0.75 cm). In other words if you kept doing averages of different samples of 100 people, you would see the averages varying from one another by around 0.3 in.

The question you then have to ask yourself is how big an effect do you want to detect? Imagine I am planning to export men's suits to Denmark from the UK. I have a pretty good idea that Danish men are taller than British men and would like to check this. If the average difference is 1 ft (30 cm) I definitely want to know, but if it is just half an inch (1.25 cm) I probably don't care.

Let's call this least difference that I care about δ (Greek letters, it's a mathematician thing), so in the example $\delta = 0.5$ in.

If I took a sample of 100 British men and 100 Danes, the standard error of the mean would be about 0.3 in. (~1 cm) for each, so it would be touch and go whether I'd be able to detect the difference. However, if I took a sample of 900 of each, then the s.e. of each average would be about 0.1 in., so I'd probably be easily able to detect differences of 0.5 in.

In general, we'd like the minimum difference we want to detect to be substantially bigger than the standard error of the mean in order to be able to detect the difference. That is: $\delta \gg \sigma/\sqrt{n}$.

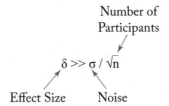

Figure 10.2: Connecting effect size (δ), noise (σ), and number (n).

Note the three elements here (Fig. 10.2):

- the effect size (δ),

- the amount of noise or uncontrolled variation (σ), and

- the number of participants, groups or trials (n).

Although the meanings of these elements vary between different kinds of data and different statistical methods, the basic triad is similar. We have seen that there are cases of such power-law distributions[2] for social network data, where the standard deviation is not well defined and other measures of spread or variation apply. With such data the exact formula changes; it is not the square root of participants that is the key factor. However, it is still the general rule that you need many more participants to get greater accuracy in measures ... but for power-law data the 'more' is even greater than squaring!

10.2.1   GENERAL STRATEGIES

Once we understand that statistical power is about the relationship between these three factors (Fig. 10.3), it becomes obvious that while increasing the number of subjects is one way to address power, it is not the only way. We can attempt to alter any one of the three, or indeed several of them, while designing our user studies or experiments.

So, we have three general strategies, for each of which we will see more detailed examples later in this section.

increase number As mentioned previously, this is the standard approach, and the only one that many people think about. However, as we have seen, the square root means that we often need a *very large increase in the number of subjects or trials* in order to reduce the variability of our results to an acceptable level. Even when you have addressed other parts of the noise–effect–number triangle, you still have to ensure you have sufficient subjects, although this should be fewer than you would need with a more naïve approach.

---

[2]Remember that this is a different use of the term 'power.'

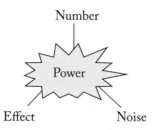

Figure 10.3: The noise–effect–number triangle.

reduce noise Noise is about variation due to factors that you do not control or about which
you have little information; we can attempt to attack either of these. First we can control
conditions to reduce the variability in our study; this is the approach usually taken in
physics and other sciences: using very pure substances with very precise instruments in
controlled environments. Alternatively, we can *measure other factors* and fit or *model the
effect of these*: for example, we might ask the participants' age, prior experience, or other
things we think may affect the results of our study.

increase effect size Finally, we can attempt to manipulate the sensitivity of our study. A notable
example of this is the photo taken from the back of the crowd at President Trump's inauguration [71]. It is very hard to assess differences in crowd size at different events using
photos taken from the front of the crowd, but photos from the back are far more sensitive.
Your studies will probably be less controversial, but you can use the same technique. Of
course, there is a corresponding danger of false baselines (Chapter 11, Section 11.2), in
that we may end up with a misleading idea of the size of effects—as noted previously, with
power comes the responsibility to report fairly and accurately.

In the rest of this chapter, we will consider strategies that address the factors of the noise–
effect–number triangle in different ways. We will concentrate first on the subjects, the users or
participants in our studies, and then on the tasks we give them to perform.

Note, the term 'subjects' when used to refer to the humans involved in a study sounds
somewhat clinical or instrumental. Some prefer the term 'user,' which is particularly appropriate
for a usability study of a device or application, or 'participant' if there is a richer engagement.
However, these terms carry their own baggage: some feel that 'user' may hold connotations of
drug misuse, and 'participant' may suggest more co-design than is actually the case. So, in the
following section, the term 'subject' is retained, as it is the most common term found in statistics,
but with the caveat that these 'subjects' are in fact people!

10.3   SUBJECTS

One set of strategies for gaining power are about the way you choose and manage your participants. We will discuss several subject-choice strategies that address all three aspects of the noise–effect–number triangle:

- more subjects or trials (increase number),

- within-subjects/within-groups studies (reduce noise),

- matched users (reduce noise), and

- targeted user group (increase effect).

10.3.1   MORE SUBJECTS OR TRIALS (INCREASE NUMBER)

First is the most common approach: to increase either the number of subjects in your experiment or study, or the number of trials or measurements you make for each one. Increasing the number of subjects helps to average out any differences between subjects due to skill, knowledge, age, or simply the fact that all of us are individuals.

Increasing the number of trials (in a controlled experiment), or measurements, can help average out within-subject variation. For example, in Fitts' Law experiments, given the same target positions, distances and sizes, each time you would get a different response time, it is the average for an individual that is expected to obey Fitts' Law.

Of course, whether you increase the number of trials or the number of subjects, the points that we've discussed already remain—you have to increase the number a lot to make a small difference in power. Remember the square root in the formula. Typically, to reduce the variability of the average by two you need to quadruple the number of subjects or trials; this sounds doable. However, if you need to decrease the variability of the average by a factor of ten then you need one hundred times as many participants or trials.

10.3.2   WITHIN-SUBJECTS/WITHIN-GROUPS STUDIES (REDUCE NOISE)

In Paul Fitts' original experiment back in 1954 [29], he had *each* subject try *all of* 16 different conditions of target size and distance, as well as 2 different stylus weights. That is he was performing what is called a within-subjects experiment.

An alternative between-subjects experiment could have taken 32 times as many participants, but had each one perform for a single condition. With enough participants this might have worked, but the number would probably have needed to be enormous.

For low-level physiological behaviour, the expectation is that even if speed and accuracy differ between people, the *overall pattern* will be the same; that is we effectively assume that between-subject variation of parameters such as Fitts' Law slope will be far less than within-subject per-trial variation.

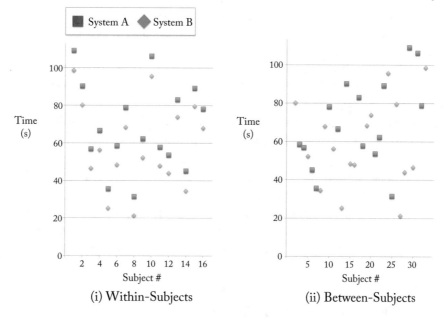

Figure 10.4: Comparing within-subjects and between-subjects studies.

Imagine we are comparing two different experimental systems A and B, and have recorded users' task completion time for each. The left-hand graph (i) in Fig. 10.4 has the results (simulated data). If you look at the difference for each subject, system A is always slower than system B; there is clearly an effect. However, imagine jumbling them up, as if you had simply asked two completely different sets of subjects, one for system A and one for system B—the difference would probably not have shown up due to the large between-subject differences. The right-hand graph (ii) in Fig. 10.4 shows the same data, but as if the data came from 32 different subjects (a between-subjects design); see how much harder it is to tell the difference between the conditions: they are masked by the large differences between individuals. In contrast, the within-subjects design effectively *cancels out these individual differences*, allowing you to see the effect of the systems.

Individual differences between people are large enough, but it is often even more challenging when we perform studies that involve groups of people collaborating. As well as the differences between the people in the groups, there will be different social dynamics at work within each group. So, when possible, performing within-groups studies is perhaps even more important; that is studies where each group performs the same tests.

However, as we have noted, increased power comes with cost; in the case of within-subjects designs the main problem is order effects, as described in Chapter 3, Section 3.2.1. The normal way to address order effects, albeit partially, is to randomise or balance the orders;

for example, you would do half the subjects in the order A–B and half in the order B–A. More complex designs might include replications of each condition such as ABBA, BAAB, ABAB, and BABA.

Fitts' original experiment did a more complex variation of this, with each participant being given the 16 conditions (of distance and size) in a random order and then repeating the task later on the same day in the opposite order.

These kinds of designs allow one to cancel out simple learning/interference effects, and even to model how large they are. However, this only works if the order effects are symmetric; if system A interferes with system B more than vice versa, there will still be underlying effects. Furthermore, it is not unusual for one of the alternatives to be the existing one that users are familiar with in the systems they use daily.

There are more sophisticated methods, for example giving each subject a lot of exposure to each system and only using the later trials to try to avoid early learning periods. For example, ten trials with system A followed by ten with system B, or vice versa, but ignoring the first five trials for each.

10.3.3   MATCHED USERS (REDUCE NOISE)

For within-subjects designs it would be ideal if we could clone users so that there would be no learning effects, but we could still compare the same user between conditions. One way to emulate this is to have different subjects for each condition, but to pair subjects who are very similar, say in terms of gender, age, or skills, and allocate one from each pair to each condition.

This is common in educational experiments, where pre-scores or previous exam results are used to rank students, and then alternate students are assigned to each condition (perhaps two ways to teach the same material). This is effectively matching on current performance.

Of course, if you are interested in teaching mathematics, then prior mathematics skills are an obvious thing to match. However, in other areas it may be less clear, and if you try to match on too many attributes you get combinatorial explosion: so many different combinations of attributes you can't find people who match on them all.

In a way, matching subjects on an attribute is like measuring the attribute and fitting a model to it, except that when you try to fit an attribute you usually need some model of how it will behave. For example, if you are looking at a teaching technique, you might assume that post-test scores may be linearly related to the students' previous year exam results. However, if the relationship is not really linear, then you might end up thinking you have found a result, when it was in fact due to your poor model. Matching subjects makes your results far more robust, requiring fewer assumptions.

A variation on matching users is to simply choose a *very narrow user group*. In some ways you are matching by making them all the same. For example, you may deliberately choose twenty-year-old college educated students … in fact you may do that by accident if you perform your experiments on psychology students! Looking back at Fitts' original paper [29], he

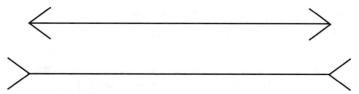

Figure 10.5: Müller–Lyer illusion.

says, "Sixteen right-handed college men served as Ss *(Subjects)*," so there is good precedent. By choosing participants of the same age and experience you get rid of a lot of the factors that might lead to individual differences. Of course there will still be personal differences due to the attributes you haven't constrained, but nonetheless you will be reducing the overall noise level.

The downside, of course, is that this then makes it *hard to generalise*. Fitts' results were for right-handed college men; do his results also hold for college women, for left-handed people, for older or younger or less well-educated men? Often it is assumed that these kinds of low-level physiological experiments are similar in form across different groups of people, but this may not always be the case.

Henrich et al. [37] reviewed a number of psychological results about cognitive and perceptual traits that were commonly assumed to be innate, independent of background and culture. The vast majority of fundamental experiments are performed on what they call WEIRD people (Western, Educated, Industrialized, Rich, and Democratic), but where there were results from people of radically different cultural backgrounds, there were often substantial differences. This even extended to low-level perception.

You may have seen the Müller–Lyer illusion (Fig. 10.5): the lower line looks longer, but in fact both lines are exactly the same length. It appears that this illusion is not innate, but is due to being brought up in an environment where there are lots of walls and rectilinear buildings. When children and adults from tribes in jungle environments are tested, they do not perceive the illusions but see the lines as the same length.

10.3.4   TARGETED USER GROUP (INCREASE EFFECT)

We can go one step further and deliberately choose a group for whom we believe we will see the maximum effect. For example, imagine that you have designed a new menu system, which you believe has a lower short-term memory requirement. If you test it on university students who are typically young and have been honing their memory skills for years, you may not see any difference. However, short-term memory loss is common as people age, so if you chose more elderly users you would be more likely to see the improvements due to your system. In different circumstances, you may deliberately choose to use novice users, because experts may be so practised on the existing system that nothing you do makes any improvement.

The choice of a targeted group means that even *small differences in your system's performance* make a *big difference for the targeted group*; that is you are *increasing the effect size*.

Just as with the choice of a narrow type of user, this may make *generalisation difficult*, only more so. With the narrow, but arbitrary group, you may argue that in fact the kind of user does not matter. However, the targeted choice of users is specifically because you think the criteria on which you are choosing them does matter and will lead to a more extreme effect.

Typically, in such cases you will use a theoretical argument in order to generalise. For example, suppose your experiment on elderly users showed a statistically significant improvement with your new system design. You might then use a combination of qualitative interviews and detailed analysis of logs to argue that the effect was indeed due to the reduced short-term memory demand of your new system. You might then argue that this effect is likely to be there for any group of users: you are reducing cognitive load, which, while not usually enough to be apparent, may well be interfering with other tasks the user is attempting to do with the system.

Alternatively, you may not be worried about generalisation: if the effect you have found is important for a particular group of users, then it will be helpful for them—you have found your market!

10.4   TASKS

As well as choosing *whom* we ask to participate in our user studies, we can manipulate *what* we ask them to do, the experimental or study tasks. We will consider four strategies:

- distractor tasks (increase effect),

- targeted tasks (increase effect),

- demonic interventions! (increase effect), and

- restricted tasks (reduce noise).

Notably missing are strategies about increasing the number of tasks. While this is possible, and indeed often desirable, the normal reason for doing it is to increase the diversity of contexts under which you study a phenomenon. Often the differences between tasks are so great that it is meaningless to do aggregate statistics in any way across tasks; instead, comparisons are made within tasks, with only broad cross-task comparisons, for example whether they all lead to improvements in performance.

Typically too, if you do want to aggregate across tasks, the models you take have to be nonlinear—if one task takes twice as long as another task, typically variations in that task between subjects or trials are also twice as large, or at least substantially larger. This often entails multiplicative rather than additive models of each task's impact.

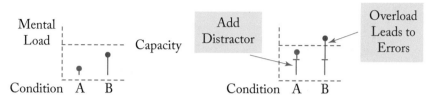

Figure 10.6: Distractor tasks make experimental load break cognitive limits.

10.4.1   DISTRACTOR TASKS (INCREASE EFFECT)

Recall that one of the strategies for choosing subjects is to select a targeted group, say novices, for whom you believe effects will be especially apparent, effects that are there for everyone, but often hidden.

Distractor tasks perform a similar role, but by manipulating the user's experimental task to make otherwise hidden differences obvious. They are commonly used in ergonomics, but less widely in HCI or user experience studies; however, they offer substantial benefits.

A distractor task is an additional task given during an experimental situation, which has the aim of saturating some aspect of the user's cognitive abilities, so that differences in load of the systems or conditions being studied become apparent. A typical example for a usability study might be to ask a subject to count backward whilst performing the primary task.

The two graphs in Fig. 10.6 show what is happening. Assume we are comparing two systems, A and B. In the example the second system has a greater mental load (graph on the left), but this is not obvious as both are well within the user's normal mental capacity.

However, if we add the distractor task (graph on the right) both tasks become more difficult, but system B with to the distractor now exceeds the mental capacity, leading to more errors, slower performance, or other signs of breakdown.

The distractor task can be arbitrary (like counting backwards), or ecologically meaningful. I first came across distractor tasks in the agricultural research institute where I used to work. There, when we were studying instruments and controls to be installed in a tractor cab, it was common to give the subjects a steering task, usually creating a straight plough furrow, while they used the equipment. By increasing the load of the steering task (for example with a faster driving simulation), there would come a point when the driver would either fail to use one of the items of equipment properly, or produce wiggly furrows. This sweet spot, when the driver was just on the point of failure, meant that even small differences in the cognitive load of the equipment under trial became apparent.

A similar HCI example of an ecologically meaningful distractor task is in mobile interface design, when users are tested using an interface whilst walking and avoiding obstacles.

Distractor tasks are particular useful when people employ coping mechanisms. Humans are resilient and resourceful; when faced with a difficult task they, consciously or unconsciously,

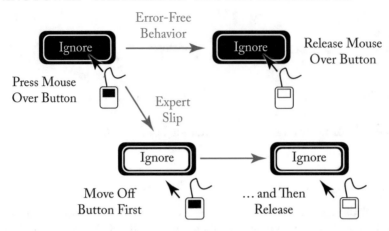

Figure 10.7: The trouble with buttons.

find ways to manage (cope). Alternatively, they may have sufficient mental resources to deal with additional effort and never even notice.

Either way the additional load is typically having an effect, even when it is not obvious. However, this hidden effect is likely to surface when the user encounters some additional load in the environment; this may be an event such as an interruption, or more long-term load, such as periods of stress or external distractions. In a way, the distractor task makes these issues obvious in the more controlled setting of your user study.

10.4.2   TARGETED TASKS (INCREASE EFFECT)

Just as we can have targeted user groups, we can also choose targeted tasks that deliberately expose the effects of our interventions. For example, if you have modified a word-processor to improve the menu layout and structure, it makes sense to have a task that involves a lot of complex menu navigation rather than simply typing.

If you have a more naturalistic task, then you may try to instrument it so that you can make separate measurements and observations of the critical parts. For example, in the word-processor your logging software might identify when menu navigation occurs for different functions, record this, and then create response-time profiles for each, so that the differences in, say, typing speed in the document itself do not drown out the impact of the menu differences.

Of course, this kind of targeting, while informative, can also be misleading, especially in a head-to-head system comparison. In such cases it is worth also trying to administer tasks where the original system is expected to perform better than your new, shiny favourite one. However, it is worth explaining that you have done this, so that reviewers do not take this as evidence that your new system is bad! (more on this in Chapter 11).

Some years ago I was involved in a very successful example of this principle. Steve Brewster was looking at possible sonic enhancement of buttons [17]. One problem he looked at was an expert slip, that is an error that only experts make, one that does not occur in novice use. In this case highly experienced users would occasionally think they had pressed a button to do something, not notice they had failed, and then only much later discover the impact (Fig. 10.7). For example, if they had cut a large body of text and thought they had pasted it somewhere, but hadn't, then the text would be lost.

Analysing this in detail, we realised that the expert user would almost certainly correctly move the mouse over the button and press it down. Most on-screen buttons allow you to cancel after this point by dragging your mouse off the button (different now with touch buttons). The expert slip appeared to be that the expert started to move the mouse button too quickly as they started to think of the next action.

A novice user would be less likely to make this error as they would be thinking more carefully about each action, whereas experts tend to think ahead to the next action. Novices would also be more likely to verify the semantic effect of their actions, so that, even if they made the slip, they would notice straight away and fix the problem. The expert slip is not so much making the error, but *failing to detect it*.

Having understood the problem, we considered a sonic enhancement (simulated click) that we believed would solve or at least reduce the problem. However, the difficulty was that this was an expert slip; it was serious when it occurred, but was very infrequent, perhaps happening only once every month or so.

Attempts to recreate it in a 10-min controlled experiment initially failed dramatically. Not only was it too infrequent to occur, but also experts behave more like novices in the artificial environment of a lab experiment, being more careful about their actions and monitoring the results.

In the current days of mass web deployment and perpetual beta, we might have tried to compare the alternatives as an A–B test, but in fact even with a massive volume of tests such an infrequent problem would be hard to detect.

Instead, we turned back to the analysis of the problem and crafted a task that created the otherwise infrequent expert slip. The final task involved typing numbers using an on-screen keyboard, clicking a button to confirm the number, and then moving to a distant button to request the next number to type. The subjects were put under time pressure (another classic manipulation to increase load), thus maximising the chance that they would slip off the confirm button whilst starting to move the mouse toward the 'next' button.

With this new task we immediately got up to a dozen missed errors in every experiment—we had recreated the infrequent expert slip with high frequency and even with novices. When the sonic enhancement was added, slips still occurred, but they were always noticed immediately, by all subjects, every time.

10.4.3 DEMONIC INTERVENTIONS! (INCREASE EFFECT)

In the extreme one can deliberately produce tasks that are plain nasty!

Some years ago I was involved in work to research natural inverse actions that provides a good example of such a task [30]. If you reverse a car using your mirrors it can initially be hard to know which way to turn the steering wheel, but if you turn and it is the wrong direction, or if you over-steer, you simply turn it the opposite way.

We wanted to create such a situation using Fitts' Law style target acquisition tasks, with various unusual mappings between two joysticks (in left and right hand) and on-screen pointers. The trouble is that when you reach for something in the real world you tend to undershoot, as overshooting would risk damaging the thing or injuring yourself. This behaviour persists even with an on-screen mouse pointer. However, we needed overshoots to be able to see what remedial action the participants would take.

In order to engineer overshoots we added a substantial random noise to the on-screen movements, so that the pointer behaved in an unpredictable way. The participants really hated us, but we did get a lot of overshoots!

Of course, creating such extreme situations means there are, yet again, problems of generalisation. This is acceptable if you are trying to understand some basic cognitive or perceptual ability, but less so if you are concerned with issues closer to real use. There is no magic bullet here. *Generalisation* is never simply about applying algorithms to data, it is always a matter of the head—*an argument based on evidence*, some statistical, some qualitative, some theoretical, some experiential.

10.4.4 RESTRICTED TASKS (REDUCE NOISE)

One of the ongoing discussions in HCI is the choice between in-the-wild studies [11, 63] or controlled laboratory experiments. Of course there are also many steps in between, from semi-realistic settings recreated in a usability lab to heavily monitored use in the real world.

In general, the more control one has over the study, the less uncontrolled variation there is and hence the noise is smaller. In a fully in-the-wild setting people typically select their own tasks, may be affected by other people around them, weather, traffic, etc. Each of these introduces variability. However, one can still exercise a degree of control, even when conducting research in the wild.

One way is to use restricted tasks. Your participants are in a real situation, their home, their office, walking down the street, but instead of doing what they like, you give them a scripted task to perform. Even though you lose some realism in terms of the chosen task, at least you still have a level of ecological validity in the environment. These controlled tasks can be interspersed with free use, although this will introduce its own potential for interference, as with within-subjects experiments.

Another approach is use a restricted device or system. For example, you might lock a mobile phone so that it can only use the app being tested. By cutting down the functionality of the device or application, you can ensure that free use is directed toward the aspects that you wish to study.

A few years ago, before phones all had GPS, one proposed mode of interaction involved taking a photograph and then having image recognition software use it to work out what you were looking at, in order to offer location-specific services such as historical information or geo-annotation [77].

Some colleagues of mine were interested in how the accuracy of the image recognition affected the user experience. In order to study this, they modified a version of their mobile tourist guide and added this as a method to enable location. The experimental system used Wizard of Oz prototyping: when the user took a photograph, it was sent to one of the research team who was able to match it against the actual buildings in the vicinity. This yielded a 100% accurate match, but the system then added varying numbers of random errors to emulate automated image recognition.

In order to ensure that the participants spent sufficient time using the image location part, the functionality of the mobile tourist guide was massively reduced, with most audio-visual materials removed and only basic textual information retained for each building or landmark. Because of this, the participants looked at many different landmarks, rather than spending a lot of time on a few, and thus ensured the maximum amount of data concerning the aspect of interest.

The rather concerning downside of this story is that many of the reviewers did not understand this scientific approach and could not understand why it did not use the most advanced media! Happily it was eventually published at mobileHCI [15].

CHAPTER 11

So what?— making sense of results

You have done your experiment or study and obtained your data; maybe you have even done some preliminary statistics. What next; how do you make sense of the results? This chapter will look at a number of issues and questions:

- eyeballing and visualising your data—finding odd cases, checking your model makes sense, and avoiding misleading diagrams;

- understanding what you have really found—is it a deep result, or merely an artefact of an experimental choice?;

- accepting the diversity of people and purposes—trying to understand not whether your system or idea is good, but who or what it is good for; and

- building for the future—ensuring your work builds the discipline, sharing data, allowing replication or meta-analysis.

Although these are questions you can ask when you are about to start data analysis, they are also the questions you should consider far earlier. One of the best ways to design a study is to imagine this situation before you start! When you think you are ready to begin recruiting participants, ask yourself, "If I have finished my study, and the results are as good as I can imagine, so what? What do I know?" It is amazing how often this leads to a complete rewriting of a survey or experimental redesign.

11.1 LOOK AT THE DATA

Look at the data; don't just add up the numbers. It seems an obvious message, but it is easy to forget when you have that huge spreadsheet and just want to throw it into SPSS or R and see whether all your hard work was worthwhile. But before you jump to work out your T-test, regression analysis or ANOVA, just stop and look.

Eyeball the raw data, as numbers, but probably in a simple graph. Don't just plot averages, initially do scatter plots of all the data points, so you can get a feel for the way it spreads. If the data is in several clumps, what do they mean? Are there anomalies or extreme values? If so, these

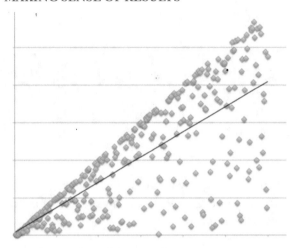

Figure 11.1: Correlated but not a simple line.

may be a sign of a fault in the experiment, maybe a sensor went wrong; or it might be something more interesting, a new or unusual phenomenon you haven't thought about.

Does the data match your model? If you are expecting linear data, does it vaguely look like that? Are you expecting the variability to stay similar for all conditions (an assumption of many tests, including regression and ANOVA)?

The graph in Fig. 11.1 is based on one I once saw in a paper (recreated here), where the authors had fitted a regression line. However, look at the data—it is not data scattered *along* a line, but rather data scattered *below* a line. The fitted line is below the max line, but the data clearly does not fit a standard model of linear fit data.

11.1.1   FITTS' LAW—JUMPING TO THE NUMBERS

A particular example in the HCI literature where researchers often forget to eyeball the data is in Fitts' Law experiments. Recall that in Fitts' original work [29] he found that the task completion time was proportional to the Index of Difficulty (IoD), which is the logarithm of the distance to target divided by the target size (with various minor tweaks!):

IoD = log_2 (distance to target/target size)

Fitts' Law has been found to hold for many different kinds of pointing tasks, with a wide variety of devices [47], and even over multiple orders of magnitude [34]. Given this, many who perform work related to Fitts' Law do not bother to separately report distance and target size effects, but instead instantly jump to calculating the IoD, assuming that Fitts' Law holds. Often the assumption proves correct … but not always.

The graph in Fig. 11.2 is based on a Fitts' Law related paper I once read. The paper was about the effects of adding noise to the pointer, as if you had a slightly dodgy mouse. Crucially,

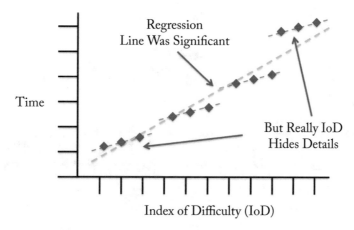

Figure 11.2: Fitts' Law data with artificial mouse error.

the noise was of a fixed size (in pixels), not related to the speed or distance of mouse movement. The dots on the graph show the averages of multiple trials on the same parameters: size, distance and the magnitude of the noise were varied. However, size and distance are not separately plotted, just the time to target against IoD.

If you understand the mechanism of Fitts' Law [4, 18], then you would expect anomalies to occur with fixed magnitude noise. In particular, if the noise is bigger than the target size you would expect to have an initial Fitts' Law movement to the general vicinity of the target, but then a Monte Carlo (utterly random) period where the noise dominates and it is pure chance when you manage to click the target.

Sure enough if you look at the graph you see small triads of points in roughly straight lines, but then the centre of each cluster of points follows a slight upward curve. The regression line is drawn, but this is clearly not simply data scattered around the line.

In fact, given an understanding of the mechanism, this is not surprising, but even without that knowledge the graph clearly shows *something* is wrong—and yet the authors never mentioned the problem.

11.1.2   BUT I DID A REGRESSION ...

Why didn't they mention it? Perhaps because they had performed a regression analysis and it had come out statistically significant. In other words, they had jumped straight for the numbers (IoD plus regression) and not properly looked at the data! They may have reasoned that if the regression is significant and the correlation coefficient strong, then the data is linear. In fact, this is *not* what regression says.

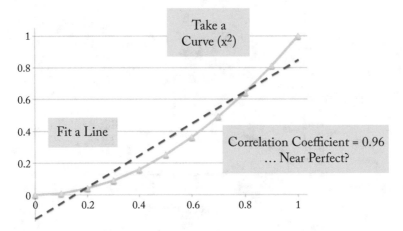

Figure 11.3: Regression line fitted to nonlinear data.

To see why, look at the data in Fig. 11.3. This is not random data from an experiment, but simply an x-squared curve. The straight line is a fitted regression line, which turns out to have a correlation coefficient of 0.96, which sounds near perfect.

There is a trend there, and the line does do a pretty good job of describing some of the change—indeed many algorithms depend on approximating curves with straight lines for precisely this reason. However, the underlying data is clearly not linear.

There are more extreme versions of this. Back in 1973, Francis Anscombe constructed four datasets, known as Anscombe's Quartet (Fig. 11.4), which have many identical statistical properties (including regression) but are clearly very different [1]. More recently, researchers at Autodesk used simulated annealing to create a scatter-plot of data that has apparently simple statistical measures but looks just like a dinosaur [51].

So next time you read about a correlation, or do one yourself, or indeed any other sort of statistical or algorithmic analysis, please, *please*, remember to *look at the data*.

11.2   VISUALISE CAREFULLY

Visualisation is a powerful tool that can help you highlight the important features in your data, but it is also dangerous and can be misleading. Visualisation is a vast topic in its own right,[1] and visualisations can be used in many ways. Crucially, they may be produced for the data consumer (your client, management, general public, illustrations in an academic article) and/or for the data analyst (including yourself) [21]. For either use, a good visualisation can highlight crucial issues and create new insights; equally a poor choice of visualisation may obscure or even mislead.

---

[1]See my own brief introduction to Information Visualisation [21] for an overview and pointers to major texts.

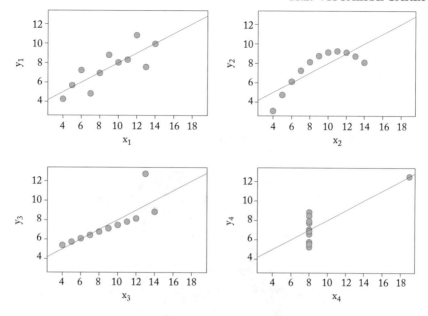

Figure 11.4: Anscombe's Quartet (source: Schutz and R team, `https://commons.wikimedia.org/w/index.php?curid=9838454`).

For initial eyeballing of raw data, you are most often using quite simple scatter plots, line graphs or histograms, so here we will deal with two choices you make about these: the baseline and the basepoint.

The first, the baseline, is about where you place the bottom of your graph: at zero, or at some other value, a 'false' baseline. The second, the basepoint, is about the left-to-right start. This is also often called a 'false origin' where the start point of a graph is not the 'true origin' of the data (0,0). In these terms the baseline is the y coordinate of the false origin and the basepoint the x coordinate.

Mathematically speaking, the x and y axes are no different, you can graph data either way, but conventionally they are used differently. Typically, the x (horizontal) axis shows the independent variable, the thing that you choose to vary experimentally (e.g., distance to target), or that is given by the world (e.g., date); the vertical, y, axis is usually the dependent variable, what you measure, for example response time or error rate. In some kinds of data, for example medical epidemiological data, or trace data from installed applications, all the data is measured equally, so the distinction is less clear. Crucially, however, some statistical methods, notably linear regression, do take this order of variables into account.

Figure 11.5: False baseline can be useful—highlighting small differences.

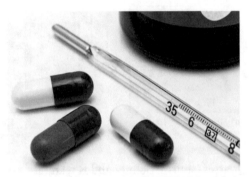

Figure 11.6: Clinical thermometer in Celsius—far easier to read than 309, 310, 311 Kelvin (source: `https://pixabay.com/photos/thermometer-temperature-fever-flu-833085/`).

11.2.1   CHOICE OF BASELINE

As noted, the baseline is about where you start, whether you place the bottom of your graph at zero or some other value: the former is arguably more 'truthful,' but the latter can help reveal differences that might get lost if the base effect is already large—think of climbing 'small' peaks near the top of Everest.

In the graph in Fig. 11.5 there is a clear change of slope. However, look more carefully at the vertical scale. The scale starts at 57.92 and the total range of the values plotted is just 0.02. This is a false baseline. Instead of starting the scale at zero, it has started at another value (in this case 57.92). The utility of this is clear. If the data had been plotted on a full scale of, say, 0–60, then even the slope would be hard to see, let alone the change in slope. Whether these small changes are important depends on the application.

Scientists use a Kelvin scale for temperature, starting at absolute zero (-273°C), but if you used this as a full scale for day-to-day measurements, even the difference between a hot summer's day and midwinter would only be about 10%; the 'false' baselines of the Celsius and Fahrenheit scales are far more useful. This is even more important in a hospital: the difference between normal temperature and high fever would be imperceptible (less than 1%) on a Kelvin

Figure 11.7: False baselines can be misleading (source: Michal Jarmoluk from Pixabay, `https://pixabay.com/photos/laboratory-analysis-chemistry-2815641/`).

scale, and medical thermometers do not even show a full Celsius range, but instead range from the mid-30s to the low-40s (Fig. 11.6).

Of course, a false baseline can also be misleading if the reader is not aware of it, making insignificant differences appear large. This may happen by accident, or it may be deliberate!

Many years ago there used to be a TV advert for a brand of painkiller, let's call it Aspradine. The TV advert showed a laboratory with impressive scientific figures in white lab coats. On the laboratory bench was a rack of four test tubes, each partly filled, to the same level, with white powder. The camera zoomed in to a view of the top portion of the test tubes, and to the words "Aspradine has 25% more active ingredient than other brands;" additional powder was poured into one, and the level rose impressively (Fig. 11.7).

Of course the words were perfectly accurate, and I'm sure they were careful to actually only add a quarter extra to the tube, but the impression given was of a much larger difference.

Recall the photographs of President Trump's inauguration, which are a high profile (and highly controversial) example of this effect. Looking at photos from the front of the crowd, it is very hard to tell the difference between different inaugurations—they all look full at the front, just as if the advert had shown only the bottom half of the test tubes. However, from the back the images clearly show the quite substantial, and not unexpected, differences between different inaugurations.[2] The downside to the use of a false baseline is that it may exaggerate effects. Just like the Aspradine advert's image of the top of the test tubes or the slope in the graph, the photos gave the misleading impression that the 2017 crowd was not just smaller than Obama's first inauguration, but in fact very small in absolute terms. Indeed, the attendance was reported

---

[2]Recall from Chapter 10 how this was used as an example of increasing sensitivity, hence making it easier to see differences.

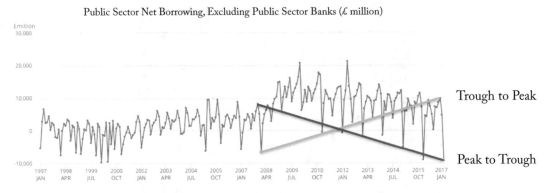

Figure 11.8: UK public sector net borrowing excluding public sector banks (£million) 1997–2017, monthly data [59] (source: `https://www.ons.gov.uk/economy/governmentpublics ectorandtaxes/publicsectorfinance/timeseries/dzls/pusf`).

by at least one news outlet at only a quarter of a million, which Trump then heard, responded to in his CIA speech … and, as they say, the rest is history.

Hopefully your research will not be as controversial, but beware. You can decide for yourself whether this sort of rhetoric is acceptable in the marketing or political arena. However, be very careful not to give misleading impressions in your academic publications!

11.2.2   CHOICE OF BASEPOINT

The graph in Fig. 11.8 shows UK public sector borrowing over a 20-year period. Imagine you want to quote a 10-year change figure. One choice might be to look at the lowest point in 2007 and compare to the highest point in 2017 (the green line). Alternatively, you might choose the highest point in 2007 and compare with the lowest in 2017. The first would suggest that there had been a massive increase in public sector borrowing; the latter would suggest a massive decrease. Both would be misleading!

In this case the data is clearly seasonal, related, one assumes, to varying tax revenues through the year, and perhaps to differing costs. Often such data is compared at a similar time each year (e.g., January–January), which would give a fairer comparison.

If the data simply varies a lot then some form of averaging is often a better approach. The graph in Fig. 11.9 shows precisely the same UK public borrowing data, but averaged over 12-month periods. Now the long-term trends are far clearer, not least the huge hike at the start of the global recession when there were large-scale bank bailouts followed by a crash in tax revenues.

You may think that, unless they were deliberately intending to deceive, no-one could make the mistake of using either of the two initial lines, since both are so clearly misleading. However, imagine you had never plotted the data and instead you were simply looking at a large spreadsheet

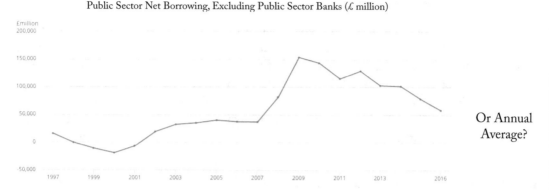

Figure 11.9: UK public sector net borrowing, excluding public sector banks (£million) 1997–2017, annual averages [59] (source: https://www.ons.gov.uk/economy/governmentpubli csectorandtaxes/publicsectorfinance/timeseries/dzls/pusf).

full of numbers. It would be easy to pick arbitrary start and end dates without realising the choice was so critical.

If this example seems contrived, a few years ago I wrote about a very similar set of data [24]. In 2016 the Scottish Labour party claimed that in Scotland the educational divide was *growing*, with access to university for those in the most deprived areas increasing by 0.8% since 2014, but those in the least deprived (most well off) growing at nearly three times that figure. In contrast, the Sottish Government (SNP) claimed that in 2006 those from the least deprived areas were 5.8 times more likely to enter university than those in the most deprived areas, whereas 10 years on, in 2016, the difference was only 3.9 times, a substantial decrease in educational inequality.

In fact, both were right; they were simply using different base years (often called base period for temporal data). The Scottish Labour party was comparing 2014 and 2016 figures, whereas the Scottish Government was looking at a 10-year difference between 2006 and 2016. There was a long-term reduction in the educational divide, but a short-term increase. Whether these different choices of base year were accidental or deliberate I do not know.

Once again, remember to *look at the data!*

11.3 WHAT HAVE YOU REALLY SHOWN?

Statistics is largely about assessing and validating measured values, but what do they actually measure? You need to *think about the conditions*: what you have really shown; ask whether your result is about an *individual or the population as a whole*; and consider whether it is about a *specific system or general properties*.

11.3.1   THINK ABOUT THE CONDITIONS

Imagine you have got good data and a gold standard p-value. You are about to write in your conclusions that using reverse alphabetic menus leads to faster access times than other layouts. However, before you commit, ask yourself, "what else might have caused this result." Maybe the tasks you used tended to include a lot of items starting with x, y, and z, for instance?

If you do find alternative explanations, you may be able to look at your data in a different way to tease out the difference between your original hypothesis and the alternatives. If you can't, that would be an opportunity to plan a new experiment that exposes the difference.

11.3.2   INDIVIDUAL OR THE POPULATION

It is easy to get confused between things that are true about your subjects and things that are true generally. Imagine you have a mobile phone app for amusement parks that offers games for families to play together while they wait in the queue for a ride. You give the app to four families, together with a small clicker device through which they are asked at regular intervals whether or not they are happy. The families visit many rides during the day and you analyse the data to see whether they are happier while waiting in queues that have an associated game, compared with queues that do not. Again you get a gold standard p-value and feel you are ready to publish.

However, given you had a small number of families, and a lot of data per family, what your statistics have really told you is that you accurately know about those four families, that those particular families are, on average, happier when they play games in the queues. However, this is simply a reliable result about a few families, *not a general result* about all families; for that you would need many more families and different statistical analysis.

This is a case where it is really important to understand what you are intending to study. Imagine that instead of four families and lots of rides per family, you had four rides and lots of families (subjects) per ride. In this case the thing you are interested in is actually the difference between the four rides: the same data would need to be interpreted very differently.

In formal experiments you may come across the terms fixed effect vs. random effect. A fixed effect is one that you choose, such as the four rides, whereas a random effect is one that might vary if you repeated the same study, such as the families you recruit, each of which may have different preferences and domestic dynamics. The former is typically something you want to find out about, whereas the latter effectively needs to be treated as an additional source of noise. However, this distinction itself depends on context. If a study was deliberately seeking to compare four specific families (maybe the Royal families of certain countries), then these would be fixed effects for that study.

11.3.3   SYSTEM VS. PROPERTIES

Perhaps even harder to spot, because it is so common, is the confusion of results about specific systems with results about the properties they embody. To illustrate this we'll look at a little story

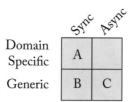

Figure 11.10: Design space.

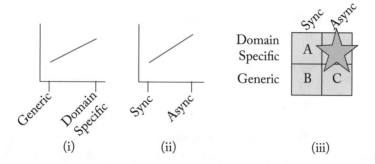

Figure 11.11: Results: (i) generic vs. domain specific; (ii) synchronous vs. asynchronous; and (iii) the interesting point in the design space.

from a few years ago. This is a particular example, but in fact it is typical of nearly every HCI paper that purports to compare some form of abstract property.

It was a major ACM conference and the presentation of what appeared to be a good empirical paper. The topic was tools to support a collaborative task. We will call the task 'X' and the study the 'task X' experiment. The researchers were interested in two main factors:

- *domain specific* for task X vs. more *generic* software and

- *synchronous* vs. *asynchronous* collaboration.

They found three pieces of existing software that covered three of the four slots in the design space (Fig. 11.10):

A – *domain specific* software, *synchronous*

B – *generic* software, *synchronous*

C – *generic* software, *asynchronous*

The experiment used sensible measures of quality for the task and had a reasonable number of subjects in each condition. Overall it seemed to be well conducted, and it had statistically significant results. The results, summarised in Fig. 11.11, showed that:

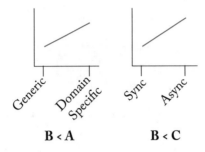

Figure 11.12: If system B simply happens to be bad …

- *domain specific* was better than *generic* (Fig. 11.11, (i)) and

- *asynchronous* was better than *synchronous* (Fig. 11.11, (ii)).

The authors concluded that what was really needed was the missing gap in the design space, asynchronous domain specific software for task X (Fig. 11.11, (iii)). One assumes that in the following year's conference they may had a paper on just such a piece of software.

There are some problems with this that are due to interaction effects: there might be some aspect to the task which means that, while domain specific synchronous software is better for task X than generic software, and asynchronous generic software is better for task X than synchronous generic software, it could still be that asynchronous domain specific software is worse. However, this is still a good place to look.

Much more importantly, if you blinked at the wrong moment in the presentation, you could easily have missed that the entire research results are potentially *completely wrong*.

Although the presentation discussed the experiment mostly in terms of the *properties*, and certainly the paper's conclusions did this, in fact these were not independently varied. Instead, *three systems* were used that *happened* to embody the relevant properties.

Let's say system B just happened to be a badly designed piece of software, nothing to do with the particular properties. During comparisons, system B would be worse than system A, which would be *interpreted* as 'domain specific is better than generic' (Fig. 11.12, left). Similarly, system B would be worse than system C, *interpreted* as 'asynchronous is better than synchronous' (Fig. 11.12, right). In reality, neither interpretation stands: system B just happens to be a poor system!

Weirdly, most experimenters would recognise an issue if there were only three users, but the problem of having a small number of pieces of software often goes unnoticed.

11.3.4   WHAT WENT WRONG?

So, what went wrong?

The experiment was run with borrowed methods from psychology, where the controlled experiments typically have a single cause and are in highly controlled environments, so that only the particular aspect being studied is varied between trials. The 'task X' experiment appears in the guise of just such a controlled experiment, varying specific qualities independently: bespoke vs. generic, synchronous vs. asynchronous.

However, interaction studies, even in lab settings, need some level of ecological validity, and indeed the systems used in the experiment were real software with all its complexities. It is the nature of such ecologically valid experiments that there are always multiple causes and open situations. Indeed, Carroll and Rosson's claims analysis [10] embraces the alternative and possibly multiple causes of the success (or failure!) of systems.

You might try to get round this issue by taking a particular system over which you have control and creating minor variants of it, embodying the various properties you'd like to compare. This is indeed often a good approach, but recall in Section 8.2 we discussed the way that the complex inter-related factors in any interface mean that it is hard to change a single property without radically redesigning large parts of the system. In this particular case, imagine taking, for example, a synchronous tool and making 'minimal' changes to create an asynchronous one. Either you'd have something so compromised it would be useless (and hence not a good comparison), or something so different it would be like having two completely different systems. The minor tweaks from domain specific to generic would of course be impossible.

The problem is that a property (such as being synchronous) is a generative artefact; it is something that is made to create other things (specific systems with that property). Other examples of generative artefacts include toolkits and design methodologies.

An obvious way to address this issue might be, for each property, to have lots and lots of systems embodying that property, just as you have lots and lots of users: effectively a larger sample of systems. However, this is typically impractical when you think of the number of user trials you would need if you wanted a reasonable number of users for each system. The closest I've encountered, usually for methodologies rather than properties, is to divide a large class of students into groups, each of which uses a different kind of method to create different designs, and then to use expert evaluation (by the course instructor or other students) for the designs themselves.

Because of the difficulties with these sample-based approaches, I have previously declared that:

the evaluation of generative artefacts is methodologically unsound. [19]

However, this does not mean that it is not possible to *validate principles*. You can use rich data: for example, collecting logs or video, using think aloud protocols, or post-task interviews. This data could be analysed to look for incidents that make it clear whether the poor performance of system B is due to the properties being studied or to other factors (such as overall poor design).

		Error Rate	
	Number	System A	System B
Novice	30	3.7%	7.4%
Expert	10	9.6%	2.7%
All	40	5.2%	6.2%

Figure 11.13: Comparing error rates for systems A and B.

In general, when you use any form of research methodology borrowed from another area, make sure you understand the assumptions behind it and modify it appropriately when you use it for yourself.

11.4   DIVERSITY: INDIVIDUAL AND TASK

It is easy, especially when promoting your own idea, to want to show that it is better than everyone else's! However, users and tasks differ from one another. Typically, a system or design property may be *useful for a particular purpose or group of users*, but not for others. If you understand this, you are in a better position to improve your research or market your system. In general, it is more important to know *who or what* something is good for.

11.4.1   DON'T JUST LOOK AT THE AVERAGE

Imagine you have run a head-to-head comparison with 40 users between two potential system designs, A and B. The data is shown in Fig. 11.13. The overall user error rates are:

system A   5.2%
system B   6.2%

They are not very different: system A is marginally better, as people have slightly fewer errors, but is that 1% difference going to change the world? However, it *is* a difference, so you go ahead and deploy system A.

However, looking more closely at the data, it just so happens that of the 40 users 30 are novices and 10 experts. Sure enough the novices have a lower error rate with system A, and indeed by a wide margin (half the error rate), but look at the expert error rates:

expert—system A   9.6%
expert—system B   2.7%   !!!!

In fact, system A is considerably worse than system B for the experts.

If this were a research setting, just looking at the averages means you have a fairly marginal result to report—yes, you might have a good p-value, but it's an effect size that will leave your

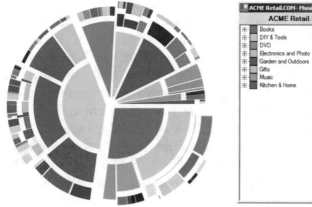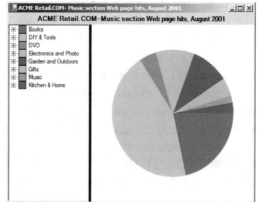

Figure 11.14: The PieTree [57] (left) fully expanded and (right) alongside a file tree.

readers yawning in their seats. However, if you look at the way this differentially affects the different groups (a) you have larger effects to report, which are also (b) far more interesting. Why do you get the different behaviour for novices and experts? What further research does this prompt?

The issue is perhaps even more critical for the usability professional. It is often easier to test a new system with novice users rather than experts; for example, you might test a financial planning application with economics students, or a diagnostic system with medical students. Novices are easier to access, and their time less costly. However, it may be that when you deploy the system, the principal user group are expert. You deployed the wrong system ... and it is worse by a large margin!

If instead of simply asking, "Is my system better?", you ask, "For whom is my system better?", then you are able to ensure that you deliver the right solution to the right people.

11.4.2   TASKS TOO

This is also true for tasks. Typically a system or interaction method is good for some purposes, but less good for others.

Figure 11.14 shows some images of the PieTree visualisation [57]. Like a TreeMap, the PieTree is a constant area visualisation for hierarchical data, in that the area of each part reflects the number or size of the items it represents. A PieTree starts as a normal pie chart of the top-level categories, but you can explode any segment to show the next level in each as smaller and smaller segments. On the left of Fig. 11.14 is a fully expanded PieTree, whereas the image on the right is unexpanded. In real use, only some segments may be expanded at any particular time, depending on where the user has drilled down. The screenshot on the right has the PieTree and a classic file tree visualisation alongside each other in a single interface.

In evaluating the PieTree several tasks were used. Some of these were extreme, following the advice on careful choice of tasks in Chapter 10. One task was focused on finding the largest items, and was deliberately designed to highlight the advantages of the PieTree over the file tree visualisation; there was an obvious strategy for the PieTree that started by drilling down into the biggest segment. However, there was also a task to find the smallest item, where there was no obvious search heuristic and everything had to be opened. For this task it was easier to scan for the smallest number in the text version of the file tree, than it was to try and work out which of the slightly differently shaped small elements in the PieTree was actually smallest.

The results were exactly as we expected, that is the PieTree visualisation was good for some kinds of tasks and the file tree for others. Having both available, as in the image on the right, was never best for any task, but was always a good second best no matter which of the visualisations 'won.'

In general, it is usually far more important to know *who or what something is good for* than some overall averaged measure. For *researchers*, knowing this is far more informative, allowing you to start to ask further questions about why certain features or properties are better. For *practitioners*, it is crucial for targeting solutions at the right people and the right problems.

11.5   MECHANISM

It is important not just to know *that* something occurs, but *how and why*. Mechanism is about understanding the steps and processes, which buttons were pressed, what screens viewed, what information was looked at and how this all comes together to create a larger phenomenon.

Crucially, understanding mechanism makes it possible to draw lessons and make predictions beyond the data available and the particular situations you have studied.

11.5.1   QUANTITATIVE AND STATISTICAL MEET QUALITATIVE AND THEORETICAL

Typically, quantitative data and statistical analysis help you understand what happens as an end-to-end phenomenon and what is *true of it as a whole*. However, they often reveal little of the processes and mechanisms by which something occurs: what, but not how and why.

In contrast, qualitative methods such as rich observations, ethnography, or post-experiment interviews are better suited to exploratory research (see Chapter 1, Section 1.4) and answering these *how and why* questions. For example, one may determine the most common ways to achieve a task by content analysis of videos or key-stroke trace data.

Theoretical understanding may help here. This can include cognitive and psychological understanding; for example, if a user is selecting a small target with an on-screen pointer, then they have to be looking directly at it, as human peripheral vision is not accurate enough for fine positioning tasks. Alternatively, it may be related to unpacking the interaction characteristics of devices or applications; for example, if someone is choosing an item from a long menu, they need to decide if the item is in the visible portion and, if not, scroll the menu, etc.

Once we have a model of how the user is behaving, we may be able to use that directly or we may use it to plan more in-depth analyses or investigations into each phase of activity.

11.5.2   GENERALISATION

When you have numerical empirical data, you often attempt to interpolate between measured values. For example, if you found that reading speed was 10% faster with a 12-point font than with a 10-point font, there is a good chance that an 11-point font will sit in between, maybe of the order of 4–6% faster. Yet this assumption may be problematic: for example, it just might be that an 11-point font pixelates badly on the particular screen resolution of the devices you are experimenting with. However, it is a reasonable heuristic.

Extrapolation is usually far harder: what about reading an 8-point font or a 32-point font or a 3-point font? However, if you understand the mechanism you can deconstruct the overall behaviour into parts that may be simple enough for you to be able to work out whether extrapolation is possible, or which can be put together in different ways to predict performance or behaviour in other contexts.

11.5.3   EXAMPLE: MOBILE FONT SIZE

As an example, we will consider an early paper on font sizes on mobile devices, which included what appeared to have been a well-conducted experiment, with statistically significant results. The paper concluded that a particular font size, let's say 12-point, was best. This sounds like a very useful piece of design advice, except for two things.

First, the result was almost certainly related to detailed device characteristics such as screen resolution: was it a 12-point font that was best, or a 12-pixel one, or simply one that did not render badly on the particular screen?

Second, the result will have been influenced by the particular task used. This involved finding items in a menu that could be paginated. Would the result hold for other tasks?

In this case it was relatively easily to work out the mechanism; the detailed steps the user would need to perform in order to complete the menu selection task are:

1. visual search of the screen to see if the target item appears,

2. if not move to next screen and try step 1 again, and

3. when it is found select the target item.

Looking through these, it seems very likely that step 1 will be easier with larger fonts until the point at which item names get too long to fit on the screen. Step 2, however, is likely to occur more frequently with larger font sizes, as there will be fewer lines and hence fewer items per screen-full, so for this step smaller fonts are bound to reduce the number of cycles. Finally, step 3 is again likely to be easier and faster with larger font sizes, whether on a touch device (larger target) or one that uses cursor keys (fewer items to move cursor through).

In summary:

Step 1	–	speed of visual search	–	large font better
Step 2	–	number of pages to scroll through	–	small font better
Step 3	–	speed of item selection	–	large font better

The optimal font size will have been a trade-off between these factors, and changes in the tasks would almost certainly have changed this figure. For example, if the search were within a very large menu, then it is likely that scrolling through pages of menu items would dominate and hence the optimal choice would be the smallest readable font. In contrast, if the number of items was always small it might be better to have a larger font, as long as they all fitted within the first screen.

Unpacking the mechanism in this way would have enabled the experimenters not only to make predictions before experimentation started, but to produce *better analyses* of their results. Indeed, they had used some form of low-level logs to produce their end-to-end times and it might have been possible to break these down into separate empirical timings for steps 1 and 3. The time for step 2 (the number of pages that needed to be scrolled through to find the target item) can be calculated precisely, with empirical data being used to determine the time taken to press the 'page down' key.

With more detailed timings, the authors could have replaced their misleading 'optimal' font size and instead provided a formula or algorithm that, given an average menu length, told you the best font size. Furthermore, other kinds of mobile task would involve steps that resemble those for the menu selection task, enabling *predictions* to be made in entirely *new contexts*.

11.6   BUILDING FOR THE FUTURE

The touchstone of valuable research is the extent to which it *builds the discipline*, so that the sum of knowledge after you have done your work is greater than it was before. How can you ensure that this happens?

11.6.1   REPEATABILITY AND REPLICATION

One important principle is repeatability, ensuring that you or others could replicate your study or experiment and get the same, or at least similar, results. At the CHI conference the RepliCHI initiative [79] held a series of workshops on this, which led to the addition of a "validation and refutation" category in some subsequent conferences.

However, true replication is hard in HCI, as it is difficult to precisely replicate the full context of even the most controlled experimental studies. The pool of subjects will differ across different institutions even if they are all university students. The experimenter usually reads some sort of protocol, or greets subjects, so slight differences in their behaviour could alter the mood of subjects. Similarly, the decoration of the room, or lack of it, light levels, etc., may all alter behaviour.

Replication can be difficult even in apparently 'physical' situations. Recall the example of 'day effects' in agricultural sprayer research, discussed in Chapter 3 (Section 3.2). Although we tried to control the spray droplets and the equipment, we still found a systematic change in measurements between days. Maybe this was some atmospheric effect, or slight difference in the equipment, we never knew.

In more ecologically valid or in-the-wild studies, replication is, of course, even harder. This does not mean you should not try to replicate, rather that you should have an awareness of the difficulties. There are things that can improve the situation.

- The first is to ensure that you are careful to *fully describe your methods* including, for example, any instructions given to participants, or data used in trials, as well as the tests used, numbers of participants, etc.

- The second is to focus on *differences or comparisons* more than absolute values. The fact that one condition is 10% faster than another in one experiment is more likely to be replicable than the exact speed of the base condition.

Understanding mechanism will help with both of these.

11.6.2   META-ANALYSIS AND OPEN SCHOLARSHIP

Meta-analysis is about using multiple studies by different groups, typically in the published literature, in order to cross-validate and find emerging patterns. Like replication, ensuring your work is amenable to meta-analysis requires you to be careful to report methods and results clearly and completely.

One way to achieve this is to put everything into the public domain, making all the materials you used open: instructions, software (if applicable), and of course the raw study data, whether this is survey reports, video, or keystroke logging, as well as derived data, all the way to the data that lies behind the graphs in your published papers.

Having this data available means that those seeking to replicate can compare different points in their process, and those seeking to do meta-analysis can calculate common statistics across different datasets, or combine the datasets as a whole. However, making your data open also means that other people can analyse it in totally unexpected ways, testing alternative models or theories, or mining it for emergent patterns.

There are ethical problems in creating open data in HCI; at very least you will usually need to anonymise the data. However, crucially you need to ensure that participants are fully aware that data may be used for purposes other than your own experiments. Often, by the time researchers come to consider publishing their data it is too late to obtain these permissions, so openness needs to be a consideration *from the very start* of your research design processes.

There are also practical problems in documenting your data well enough. During my thousand-mile walk around Wales in 2013 I collected copious data, from bio-data to blogs [22, 23]. When I had finished the walk and wanted to make this data available as a public open science resource I found I had to learn a whole new skill of documenting the data to ensure that those using it could do so without necessarily consulting me. In part, this was technical documentation: each field had to be described carefully; it was also about making sure that the user of the data would know exactly how it had been collected. Happily, the time and care spent on this have paid off and I often hear of people using the data who have never been in touch with me to ask questions about it.

There are also broader cultural issues around the use of data. The UK has a periodic research assessment exercise, which grades the research in every academic institution. During the REF 2014 exercise, the humanities panel included curated datasets as one of their categories of research output, but the science and engineering panel did not. It is not that STEM researchers do not think that data is *valuable*, but it is not *valued*, in the sense that careers, promotion and esteem are attached to the analysis and implications of data, not the meticulous work of data collection itself.

Happily, this is now changing. Many journals now mandate that data be provided for any publication, and many universities are establishing data repositories alongside those for publications themselves. Additionally, a number of data journals have appeared over recent years. Some are targeted at specific areas; some are more general, such as Elsevier *Data in Brief* (ISSN 2352-3409), Nature *Scientific Data* (ISSN 2052-4463), and MDPI *Data* (ISSN 2306-5729).

Despite the barriers, making your data available to the world is of immense value. You have often expended great effort in gathering it, it is surely worthwhile to see it reused by others … and, of course, by doing so you are doing your small part to build a stronger, greater and more robust discipline.

CHAPTER 12

Moving forward: the future of statistics in HCI

The use of statistics in HCI goes back to its first days, reflecting the methodological influence of psychology in the early discipline. Since that time there have been occasional debates over the ideal nature, or indeed value, of statistics [8, 26, 33, 44] and recent automated literature research suggests that over half the papers in the annual ACM CHI conference proceedings report some form of statistics, although some of this may be of questionable quality [6].

As we have already seen, all design and all science ultimately comes from our heads, a combination of personal experience, empirical data and rigorous reasoning. There was a time when the authors of nearly every paper felt they needed to perform a quantitative usability evaluation. Happily this is no longer the case, with the growth in understanding of the rich ways in which different kinds of intervention need to be assessed [32, 60, 61]. We noted in Chapter 11 (Section 11.3.4) that empirical evaluation is only one way to validate our work, to tell whether it really has some true impact; in practice some level of judgment is always required [19].

So, there has always been some discussion about the appropriate role of statistics in HCI. However, the level of discourse has increased markedly over recent years, kindled by the wider discourse about replication and rigour of statistics in other disciplines.

12.1 POSITIVE CHANGES

Most of the effects of this growing discourse have been very positive.

The "RepliCHI" workshops[1] in 2013 and 2014 [78] led to long-term changes in the ACM CHI Conference publication guidelines, and a survey of articles in major HCI venues suggested that replication is more common than at first appears, and that small changes in practices could significantly increase the level of reported replication [38].

The series of workshops on "Transparent Statistics in Human–Computer Interaction[2]" is creating guidance on best practice reporting of statistics [6, 67, 69] and, perhaps more importantly, fuelling an ongoing discourse and community around these issues [25, 28].

Both of these initiatives connect to broader initiatives for more open and transparent scientific practices. Within the HCI community these have included proposals [13] for the pre-

---

[1] http://www.replichi.com/
[2] https://transparentstatistics.org/

registration of studies (see Chapter 8, Section 8.1.5)) and for the publication of all research outputs where possible, including data and code [12, 27, 68].

12.2   WORRYING TRENDS

However, not all the effects have been quite so positive.

There are some who have used the statistical crisis as an excuse to avoid using statistics where they are appropriate and necessary. As noted at the beginning of the book, if you are looking at numbers and making some form of general inference, you are doing statistics, no matter how informally. Where the numbers are overwhelming, for example 187 out of 200 participants, then you may not need to do any formal analysis or test. Where they are less clear cut, say 8 out of 10, and yet you are making general statements of number such as "most people do X" (even if merely implied by "most participants …"), then you should be reaching for more explicit statistics. Remember, the correct response to bad statistics is not less statistics, but better statistics.

Another potential problem is the temptation to say "old stats is in crisis, let's try something new." As discussed in Chapter 9 (Section 9.2.1), most of the problems highlighted in recent years have been well known for at least 40 years and have equally well-known solutions. In most cases there are equivalent problems in alternative techniques, but they are often less recognised, such as the tendency to ignore cherry picking dangers in Bayesian statistics (see Chapter 8, Section 8.1).

A nice example of this is the suggestion to make meta-analysis easier in HCI by using Bayesian statistics [46] discussed in Chapter 7 (Section 7.5). At first this sounds compelling. It is possible to combine the results of multiple papers that have used traditional hypothesis testing, but the process is complex. In contrast, the suggestion is that the posterior probabilities of some effect calculated in one study can be used as a prior for the next. Over time the chain of evidence may allow stronger statements to be made, or alternatively the weakness of initial evidence to become apparent. However, this overlooks the problems of producing *exact* replication within HCI studies. More crucially, as we saw, it increases the potential of accidentally double counting initial evidence. A better approach is to ensure that all data and analysis are open, and hence allow not only future meta-analysis, but also alternative analysis of your data by others.

12.3   BIG DATA AND MACHINE LEARNING

The vast amounts of data now available allow us to study phenomena in a way that would have been impossible only a few years ago. However, the analysis of such data, whether through visualisation and statistical analysis, or through machine learning techniques, can also open up the potential to engage unintentionally in many of the cherry picking practices we discussed in Chapter 8 (Section 8.1).

Simple A–B testing is safe, trying out a fixed modification. The numbers are usually so large that no formal statistics are needed beyond calculating averages. The issue is rarely whether an effect seen is real or not (statistically significant or sufficient Bayesian evidence), but whether it matters (size of effect).

In contrast, when a machine learning algorithm is applied to very large datasets, it effectively tries out thousands of potential rules (hypotheses) and reports only the successful ones; similarly when you visualise large quantities of data you only test the patterns you spot. When dealing with such data, it would be impossible to pre-register all one's potential analyses. However, it is essential to be aware of the dangers of the multiple potential alternative rules or patterns and adjust your analyses accordingly. The details of how to do this depend on the precise methods and sometimes the tools used will perform an appropriate correction or control. If there are no such explicit corrections, do check with those who are expert in the methods, or judge the reliability of the outputs accordingly.

12.4   LAST WORDS

We are at an exciting time when the combination of computational power and available data enable systems and research that were impossible until very recently. This will have a profound impact on our discipline. I was talking to a senior UX researcher from one of the main global software companies; he said that within his organisation many of the fine UX decisions that were once made by designers are now made by machines, using A–B testing to determine questions such as placement, colours and sizes. The focus for the UX designer is no longer the minor details of interfaces, but larger and deeper questions about the fundamental purpose of systems.

Tools such as R mean that many of the traditional skills learnt in statistics courses are a thing of the past. You do not need to know the precise algorithm for calculation of a t-test or regression line, the computer just does it. Furthermore, the methods of statistics used to be designed to be easy to calculate by hand; these constraints have been broken allowing, for example, precise p-values rather than tables of critical values and simulation methods.

The challenge today is not calculating statistics, but understanding them. I hope this book has helped you along that journey.

I hope also that, in coming years, as well as tools to help calculate statistics, there will be tools to aid with this understanding that are framed in the language of the user ... that is you! There are already promising signs such as work on interactive statistical reports [25, 56] and tools to help explore potential statistical analyses [49, 70]. As well as understanding statistics yourself, perhaps you will even design the next generation of tools that will help others.

Bibliography

[1] Anscombe, F. J. (1973). Graphs in statistical analysis. *American Statistician*, 27:17–21. DOI: 10.2307/2682899. 124

[2] APA (2010). *Publication Manual of the American Psychological Association*, 6th ed. http://www.apastyle.org/manual/ DOI: 10.1037/0000165-000. 100

[3] Baker, M. (2016). Statisticians issue warning over misuse of P values. *Nature*, 531:151. DOI: 10.1038/nature.2016.19503. 98

[4] Beamish, D., Bhatti, S. A., MacKenzie, I. S., and Wu, J. (2006). Fifty years later: A neurodynamic explanation of Fitts' law. *Journal of the Royal Society Interface*, 3(10):649–654. DOI: 10.1098/rsif.2006.0123. 123

[5] Bechara, A., Damasio, H., Tranel, D., and Damasio, A. R. (1997). Deciding advantageously before knowing the advantageous strategy. *Science*, 275(5304):1293–95. DOI: 10.1126/science.275.5304.1293. 2

[6] Besançon, L. and Dragicevic, P. (2019). The continued prevalence of dichotomous inferences at CHI. In *Extended Abstracts of the CHI Conference on Human Factors in Computing Systems (CHI EA'19)*, alt14:11, ACM, New York. DOI: 10.1145/3290607.3310432. 141

[7] Bickel, P., Hammel, E., and O'Connell, J. (1975). Sex bias in graduate admissions: Data from Berkeley. *Science*, 187(4175):398–404. http://www.jstor.org/stable/1739581 DOI: 10.1126/science.187.4175.398. 35

[8] Cairns, P. (2007). HCI...not as it should be: Inferential statistics in HCI research. In *Proc. of the 21st British HCI Group Annual Conference on People and Computers: HCI...but not as we know it—Volume 1 (BCS-HCI'07)*, 1:195–201, British Computer Society, Swinton, UK. 98, 141

[9] Cairns, P. (2019). *Doing Better Statistics in Human-Computer Interaction*, Cambridge University Press. DOI: 10.1017/9781108685139. xvii

[10] Carroll, J. M. and Rosson, M. B. (1992). Getting around the task-artifact cycle: How to make claims and design by scenario. *ACM Transactions on Information Systems*, 10(2):181–212. DOI: 10.1145/146802.146834. 133

[11] Chamberlain, A. and Crabtree, A. (2019). *Into the Wild: Beyond the Design Research Lab*, Springer. DOI: 10.1007/978-3-030-18020-1. 118

[12] Chuang, L. L. and Pfeil, U. (2018). Transparency and openness promotion guidelines for HCI. In *Extended Abstracts of the CHI Conference on Human Factors in Computing Systems (CHI EA'18)*, SIG04:4, ACM, New York. DOI: 10.1145/3170427.3185377. 142

[13] Cockburn, A., Gutwin, C., and Dix, A. (2018). HARK no more: On the preregistration of CHI experiments. *Proc. of ACM CHI Conference on Human Factors in Computing Systems*, CHI Best Paper Award. Montreal, Canada. (in press). DOI: 10.1145/3173574.3173715. 83, 141

[14] Cox, R. (1946). Probability, frequency, and reasonable expectation. *American Journal of Physics*, 14(2):1–13. DOI: 10.1119/1.1990764. 8

[15] Davies, N., Cheverst, K., Dix, A., and Hesse, A. (2005). Understanding the role of image recognition in mobile tour guides. *Proc. of Mobile HCI'2005*, pp. 191–198, ACM Press. https://alandix.com/academic/papers/MobileHCI2005-camera/ DOI: 10.1145/1085777.1085809. 119

[16] Dienes, Z. (2014). Using Bayes to get the most out of non-significant results. *Frontiers in Psychology*, 5(781). DOI: 10.3389/fpsyg.2014.00781. 100

[17] Dix, A. and Brewster, S. A. (1994). Causing trouble with buttons. *Ancilliary Proceedings of HCI'94*, Glasgow, Scotland. D. England, Ed., https://alandix.com/academic/papers/buttons94/ 117

[18] Dix, A. (2003/2005). *A Cybernetic Understanding of Fitts' Law*, HCI book online. http://www.hcibook.com/e3/online/fitts-cybernetic/ 123

[19] Dix, A. (2008). Theoretical analysis and theory creation, Chapter 9 in *Research Methods for Human-Computer Interaction*, Cairns, P. and Cox, A. Eds., Cambridge University Press, pp. 175–195. http://www.alandix.com/academic/papers/theory-chapter-2008/ 133, 141

[20] Dix, A. (2011). *Are Five Users Enough?*, HCI book online. http://www.hcibook.com/e3/online/are-five-users-enough/ 13

[21] Dix, A. (2011). *Information Visualization*, PROMISE Winter School 2012, *Information Retrieval Meets Information Visualization*, Zinal, Valais, Switzerland, January 23–27, 2012. https://www.alandix.com/academic/teaching/Promise2012/ 124

[22] Dix, A. (2013). The walk: Exploring the technical and social margins. *Keynote APCHI/India HCI*, Bangalore, India. https://www.alandix.com/academic/talks/APCHI-2013/ 139

[23] Dix, A. (2013). *Alan Walks Wales—Data*. https://alanwalks.wales/data/ 139

[24] Dix, A. (2016). *The Educational Divide—Do Numbers Matter?* https://alandix.com/bl og/2016/12/24/the-educational-divide-do-numbers-matter/ 129

[25] Dragicevic, P., Jansen, Y., Sarma, A., Kay, M., and Chevalier, F. (2019). Increasing the transparency of research papers with explorable multiverse analyses. In *Proc. of the CHI Conference on Human Factors in Computing Systems (CHI'19)*, 65:15, ACM, New York. DOI: 10.1145/3290605.3300295. 141, 143

[26] Dunlop, M. and Baillie, M. (2009). Paper rejected (p>0.05): An introduction to the debate on appropriateness of null-hypothesis testing. *IJMHCI*, 1:86–93. DOI: 10.4018/jmhci.2009070108. 141

[27] Echtler, F. and Häußler, M. (2018). Open source, open science, and the replication crisis in HCI. In *Extended Abstracts of the CHI Conference on Human Factors in Computing Systems (CHI EA'18)*, alt02:8, ACM, New York. DOI: 10.1145/3170427.3188395. 142

[28] Feger, S. S., Dallmeier-Tiessen, S., Schmidt, A., and Woźniak, P. W. (2019). Designing for reproducibility: A qualitative study of challenges and opportunities in high energy physics. In *Proc. of the CHI Conference on Human Factors in Computing Systems (CHI'19)*, 455:14, ACM, New York. DOI: 10.1145/3290605.3300685. 141

[29] Fitts, P. M. (1954). The information capacity of the human motor system in controlling the amplitude of movement. *Journal of Experimental Psychology*, 47(6):381–391. DOI: 10.1037/h0055392. 110, 112, 122

[30] Ghazali, M., Dix, A., and Gilleade, K. (2015). The relationship of physicality and its underlying mapping. In *4th International Conference on Research and Innovation in Information Systems*, Malacca (best paper award). Also published in *ARPN Journal of Engineering and Applied Science*. https://alandix.com/academic/papers/ICRIIS-2015-physicality/ 118

[31] Gladwell, M. (2007). *Blink*, Little, Brown and Co. http://gladwell.com/blink/the-second-mind/ 1

[32] Greenberg, S. and Buxton, B. (2008). Usability evaluation considered harmful (some of the time). In *Proc. of the SIGCHI Conference on Human Factors in Computing Systems (CHI'08)*, pp. 111–120, ACM, New York. DOI: 10.1145/1357054.1357074. 141

[33] Caine, K. (2016). Local standards for sample size at CHI. In *Proc. of the CHI Conference on Human Factors in Computing Systems (CHI'16)*, pp. 981–992, ACM, New York. DOI: 10.1145/2858036.2858498. 141

[34] Guiard, Y., Beaudouin-Lafon, M., and Mottet, D. (1999). Navigation as multiscale pointing: Extending Fitts' model to very high precision tasks. In *Proc. ACM Human Factors in Computing Systems, CHI'99*, pp. 450-457, ACM, Pittsburgh. DOI: 10.1145/302979.303128. 122

[35] Guo, M. and Heitjan, D. F. (2010). Multiplicity-calibrated Bayesian hypothesis tests. *Biostatistics*, 11(3):473–483, Oxford, England. DOI: 10.1093/biostatistics/kxq012. 81

[36] Hájek, A. (2019). Interpretations of probability, *The Stanford Encyclopedia of Philosophy* (Fall 2019 Edition), Zalta, E. N. Ed. https://plato.stanford.edu/archives/fall 2019/entries/probability-interpret/ 72

[37] Henrich, J., Heine, S., Norenzayan, A. (2010). The weirdest people in the world? *Behavioral and Brain Sciences*, 33(2–3):61–83; discussion 83–135. DOI: 10.1017/s0140525x0999152x. 37, 113

[38] Hornbæk, K., Sander, S. S., Bargas-Avila, J. A., and Simonsen, J. G. (2014). Is once enough?: on the extent and content of replications in human-computer interaction. In *Proc. of the SIGCHI Conference on Human Factors in Computing Systems (CHI'14)*, pp. 3523–3532, ACM, New York. DOI: 10.1145/2556288.2557004. 141

[39] Hudson, J., Dix, A., and Parkes, A. (2004). User interface overloading, a novel approach for handheld device text input. *Proc. of HCI*, pp. 69–85, Springer-Verlag. http://www.alandix.com/academic/papers/HCI2004-overloading/ DOI: 10.1007/1-84628-062-1_5. 67

[40] Jaynes, E. T. (1988). How does the brain do plausible reasoning? In *Maximum-Entropy and Bayesian Methods in Science and Engineering (1)*, Erickson, G. J. and Smith, C. R., Eds., pp. 1–24, Kluwer Academic Publishers. DOI: 10.1007/978-94-009-3049-0. 8

[41] Jaynes, E. T. (2003). *Probability Theory: The Logic of Science*, Cambridge University Press. DOI: 10.1017/cbo9780511790423. 8

[42] Jeffreys, H. (1961). *Theory of Probability*, Oxford University Press, Oxford, UK. 76

[43] Kahneman, D. (2011). *Thinking, Fast and Slow*, Macmillan. 1

[44] Kaptein, M. and Robertson, J. (2012). Rethinking statistical analysis methods for CHI. In *Proc. of the SIGCHI Conference on Human Factors in Computing Systems (CHI'12)*, pp. 1105–1114, ACM, New York. DOI: 10.1145/2207676.2208557. 141

[45] Kass, R. E. and Raftery, A. E. (1995). Bayes factors. *Journal of the American Statistical Association*, 90(430):791. DOI: 10.1080/01621459.1995.10476572. 76

[46] Kay, M., Nelson, G., and Hekler, E. (2016). Researcher-centered design of statistics: Why Bayesian statistics better fit the culture and incentives of HCI. *CHI*, pp. 4521–4532, ACM. DOI: 10.1145/2858036.2858465. 78, 98, 142

[47] MacKenzie, I. S., Sellen, A., Buxton, W. A. S. (1991). A comparison of input devices in elemental pointing and dragging tasks. *Proc. of the ACM CHI Conference on Human Factors in Computing Systems*, pp. 161–166. DOI: 10.1145/108844.108868. 122

[48] Magritte, R. (1929). *La Trahison des Images*. (The Treachery of Images). Painting. https://en.wikipedia.org/wiki/The_Treachery_of_Images 72

[49] Martens, J.-B. (2019). Insights in experimental data through intuitive and interactive statistics. In *Extended Abstracts of the CHI Conference on Human Factors in Computing Systems (CHI EA'19)*, C09:4, ACM, New York. DOI: 10.1145/3290607.3298808. 143

[50] Marty, P. F. and Twidale, M. B. (2005). Extreme discount usability engineering. *Technical Report*. http://citeseerx.ist.psu.edu/viewdoc/summary?doi=10.1.1.74.3702 13

[51] Matejka, J. and Fitzmaurice, G. (2017). Same stats, different graphs: Generating datasets with varied appearance and identical statistics through simulated annealing. In *Proc. of the CHI Conference on Human Factors in Computing Systems (CHI'17)*. pp. 1290–1294, ACM, New York. DOI: 10.1145/3025453.3025912. 124

[52] McGinn, J. and Chang, A. R. (2013). RITE+Krug: A combination of usability test methods for agile design. *Journal of Usability Studies*, 8(3):61–68. 13

[53] Medlock, M. C., Wixon, D., Terrano, M., Romero, R., and Fulton, B. (2002). Using the RITE method to improve products: A definition and a case study. Presented at the Usability Professionals Association, Orlando, FL. 13

[54] Nielsen, J. and Landauer, T. (1993). A mathematical model of the finding of usability problems. *INTERACT/CHI'93*, pp. 206–213, ACM. DOI: 10.1145/169059.169166. 13

[55] Nielsen, J. (2012). *How Many Test Users in a Usability Study?*. NN/g Norman–Nielsen Group. https://www.nngroup.com/articles/how-many-test-users/ 13

[56] Nolan, D. and Lang, D. T. (2007). Dynamic, interactive documents for teaching statistical practice. *International Statistical Review*, 75(3):295–321. DOI: 10.1111/j.1751-5823.2007.00025.x. 143

[57] O'Donnell, R., Dix, A., and Ball, L. (2006). Exploring the PieTree for representing numerical hierarchical data. *Proc. of HCI, People and Computers XX–Engage*, pp. 239–254, Springer. http://www.alandix.com/academic/papers/HCI2006-PieTree/ DOI: 10.1007/978-1-84628-664-3_18. 135

150   BIBLIOGRAPHY

[58] Office of National Statistics (2014). *Sustainable Development Indicators.* `http://webarchive.nationalarchives.gov.uk/20160105183323/` `http://www.ons.gov.uk/ons/rel/wellbeing/sustainable-development-indicators/july-2014/sustainable-development-indicators.html` 45

[59] Office of National Statistics (2017). Public sector net borrowing, excluding public sector banks (£million). `https://www.ons.gov.uk/economy/governmentpublicsectorandtaxes/publicsectorfinance/timeseries/dzls/pusf` 128, 129

[60] Olsen, D. R. Jr. (2007). Evaluating user interface systems research. In *Proc. of the 20th Annual ACM Symposium on User Interface Software and Technology (UIST'07)*, pp. 251–258, ACM, New York. DOI: 10.1145/1294211.1294256. 141

[61] Remy, C., Bates, O., Mankoff, J., and Friday, A. (2018). Evaluating HCI research beyond usability. In *Extended Abstracts of the CHI Conference on Human Factors in Computing Systems (CHI EA'18)*, SIG13:4, ACM, New York. DOI: 10.1145/3170427.3185371. 141

[62] Robertson, J. and Kaptein, M. (Eds.) (2016). *Modern Statistical Methods for HCI*, Springer. DOI: 10.1007/978-3-319-26633-6. xvii

[63] Rogers, Y. and Marshall, P. (2017). *Research in the Wild*. Synthesis Lectures on Human-Centered Informatics, Morgan & Claypool. DOI: 10.2200/s00764ed1v01y201703hci037. 118

[64] RSS. (2015). Statistician or statistical scientist? An interview with RSS president Peter Diggle. *StatsLife, Royal Statistical Society.* `https://www.statslife.org.uk/features/2822-statistician-or-statistical-scientist-an-interview-with-rss-president-peter-diggle` 102

[65] Sense about Science. (2010). Making sense of statistics. Sense about science. In *Royal Statistical Society.* `http://senseaboutscience.org/activities/making-sense-of-statistics/` 102

[66] Simonsohn, U., Nelson, L. D., and Simmons, J. P. (2014). P-curve: A key to the file-drawer. *Journal of Experimental Psychology: General*, 143(2):534–547. DOI: 10.1037/a0033242. 87

[67] Transparent statistics in human–computer interaction working group. (2019). *Transparent Statistics Guidelines.* DOI: 5281/zenodo.2226616. 141

[68] Wacharamanotham, C., Eisenring, L., Haroz, S., Echtler, F. (2019). Transparency of CHI research artifacts: Results of a self-reported survey. *OSF Preprints.* `https://osf.io/3bu6t/` DOI: 10.31219/osf.io/3bu6t. 142

[69] Wacharamanotham, C., Kay, M., Haroz, S., Guha, S., and Dragicevic, P. (2018). Special interest group on transparent statistics guidelines. In *Extended Abstracts of the CHI Conference on Human Factors in Computing Systems (CHI EA'18)*, SIG08:4, ACM, New York. DOI: 10.1145/3170427.3185374. 141

[70] Wacharamanotham, C., Subramanian, K., Völkel, S. T., and Borchers, J. (2015). Statsplorer: Guiding novices in statistical analysis. In *Proc. of the 33rd Annual ACM Conference on Human Factors in Computing Systems*, pp. 2693–2702, ACM. DOI: 10.1145/2702123.2702347. 143

[71] Wallace, T., Yourish, K., and Griggs, T. (2017). Trump's inauguration vs. Obama's: Comparing the crowds. *New York Times*. https://www.nytimes.com/interactive/2017/01/20/us/politics/trump-inauguration-crowd.html 109

[72] Ward, M. (2002). *Universality: The Underlying Theory Behind Life, The Universe and Everything*, Pan. 51

[73] Wasserstein, R. L. and Lazar, N. A. (2016). The ASA's statement on p-values: Context, process, and purpose. *The American Statistician*, 70(2):129–133. DOI: 10.1080/00031305.2016.1154108. 101

[74] Wasserstein, R. L., Schirm, A. L., and Lazar, N. A. (2019). Moving to a world beyond "$p < 0.05$". *The American Statistician*, 73(sup1):1–19. DOI: 10.1080/00031305.2019.1583913. 101

[75] Wetzels, R., Matzke, D., Lee, M. D., Rouder, J. N., Iverson, G. J., and Wagenmakers, E.-J. (2011). Statistical evidence in experimental psychology. *Perspectives on Psychological Science*, 6:291. DOI: 10.1177/1745691611406923. 76, 77

[76] Wikipedia (2017). Bayes factor. https://web.archive.org/web/20170722072451/https://en.wikipedia.org/wiki/Bayes_factor 100

[77] Wilhelm, A., Takhteyev, Y., Sarvas, R., Van House, N. and Davis. M. (2004). Photo annotation on a camera phone. *Extended Abstracts of CHI*, pp. 1403–1406, ACM Press, Vienna, Austria. DOI: 10.1145/985921.986075. 119

[78] Wilson, M. L., Chi, E. H., Reeves, S., and Coyle, D. (2014). RepliCHI: the workshop II. In *Extended Abstracts on Human Factors in Computing Systems (CHI EA'14)*, pp. 33–36, ACM, New York. DOI: 10.1145/2559206.2559233. 141

[79] Wilson, M. (2011–2019). RepliCHI: Revisiting HCI findings. 519(7541):9. http://www.replichi.com 138

[80] Woolston, C. (2015). Psychology journal bans p-values. *Nature News, Research Highlights: Social Selection*, 519(7541):9. http://www.nature.com/news/psychology-journal-bans-p-values-1.17001 DOI: 10.1038/519009f. 100

Author's Biography

ALAN DIX

Alan Dix is the Director of the Computational Foundry, Swansea University, Wales. He is well known for an HCI textbook and research in HCI including CSCW, mobile interfaces, technical creativity, and some of the earliest work on privacy and the ethical implications of intelligent data processing. More recent work includes community engagement, especially in rural areas, and his thousand-mile research walk around Wales, which generated substantial quantitative and qualitative open research data, from blogs to biodata.

Before he was in HCI, Alan was a mathematician, including representing the UK in the International Mathematical Olympiad. He has practised as a professional statistician and applied mathematician including work on modelling agricultural crop sprays, medical statistics, and undersea cable detection. Within HCI these skills have been applied in his foundational work on formal methods for interactive systems, the use of Bayesian techniques in education, random sampling for visualisation of big data and uncertainty, and analysis of potential bias against human/applied areas in REF, the UK research assessment exercise.

This unusual combination of skills and experience gives Alan unique insight into the challenges and problems of applying statistics to HCI data.

Index